absolutely fabulous

ELY

jennifer saunders

ULOUS

B

BBC BOOKS

This book is published to accompany the
television series entitled *Absolutely Fabulous*
which was first broadcast in Autumn 1992
Published by BBC Books,
a division of BBC Enterprises Limited,
Woodlands, 80 Wood Lane
London W12 0TT

First published 1993
Reprinted 1993
© Mr & Mrs Monsoon Ltd 1993
ISBN 0 563 36976 0

Designed by Hammond Hammond

Photographs © BBC

Set in Monotype Bembo by Selwood Systems,
Midsomer Norton
Printed and bound in Great Britain by
Butler & Tanner Ltd, Frome, Somerset
Colour separation by Dot Gradations Ltd,
Near Chelmsford
Jacket printed by Lawrence Allen Ltd,
Weston-super-Mare

Contents

Introduction

i HAVE TO thank Ruby Wax.

That over, I bet I know what you're longing to know. How did *Absolutely Fabulous* come together? It is a question that I am often stopped and asked in the street (I am no longer able to go shopping at Tesco, due to my fame. Thank God!). Sometimes people follow me down the road, tugging at my sleeve in a rather humiliating and Dickensian way, (Marks & Spencer is fine, but then there is more to look at and a better class of person generally, often I am not the only celebrity! Why just the other day I was discussing the merits of baby carrots and pre-cut salad bags with the likes of Pat Hodge and Heather Scott, of Sky TV fame) and they persist in shouting, 'Dawn French! Oh no, it's the other one wot is her friend, that mad bint in that thing with the gorgeous Joanna Lumley. How's Dawn then? Why i'nt she in it? How's that then?'

Ah me, the price of fame. Obviously it's embarrassing, but I am forced to reply, somewhat along these lines, 'She's not in it because she was too old for the part, alright?' *C'est dommage, ma que sera, sera,* as they say. As luck would have it, though, the lovely Julia Sawalha, of *Press Gang* and *Every Second Counts* fame, was ready to step into those shoes and they fitted like a glove.

The casting of most of the other main roles was as easy and trouble free. The lovely June Whitfield, of Terry fame, I had always wanted as my mother. She is also tremendously funny, although I hadn't really seen any of the other parts as funny. You see, I think it's confusing for an audience, they're left thinking, 'Oh, hang on, I thought Jennifer Saunders was supposed to be the funny one here, since she bothered to write it and star in it, and now everybody else is trying to get in on the act. What the hell is going on!' I tried to explain this to

June, but it was like talking to a brick wall. Heigh-ho!

Then came Bubble, and the gorgeous and much-in-demand actress (I'm not complaining, but I could play an anorexic single parent on heroin with my eyes closed) Jane Horrocks, (I'm just fed up of the pigeon-holing in this business) of huge fame, was perfect for the part despite the fact that she is not at all stupid in real life.

The biggest problem arose with the casting of the Patsy part. I always felt that there was someone out there who was perfect for the role. I still do. Eventually, though, a decision had to be made and it came down to this;

Jennifer Saunders

Dear Miss ~~Rigg Blackman Thorson Rice~~ . Lumly
I hope you are well. I am an great admirer
of your work\s .
I have seen all your shows from SAPPHIRE to STEEL
and havegreat pleasure therfore in
inviting you to take the part of Patsy
Stone in my new Situation Comedt , working
tit,le " Gosh , I'm Funny! "
It is nearly thr lead and with your
~~talent\looks\comedy experience~~ HAIR I feel you
are perfect .
We would lik to meet you at our
convenience and ask you to read.

Yours sincerely\ faithfully

[signature]   (writer\star)

ps. Please send recent photo

JOANNA LUMLEY

Dear Jennifer,
 What luck! I'm suddenly free for a year or more and so can accept your invitation to star with you. Yet again I find myself in the unfortunate predicament of having spilt acid on my photographs so I've enclosed some recent artist's impression of me - Would love to sing or read for you.
As Sapphire always said 'Steel - I'm getting something here'
 yours sincerely
 Joanna Lumley.
P.S. Can be reached 24 hrs a day on my bleeper. Which I've just bought.

JOANNA LUMLEY

not frizzy hair

huge thick lashes real

Julia Roberts type mouth always half-smiling

amazingly charming and unscraggy neck

So there you have it. *C'est la vie* and the rest is history.

Characters

EDINA In her very late thirties. Two children both by different husbands. Son at university. Daughter at school. Lives life at a manic pace. Is neurotic, successful, in charge of her own company which is a Public Relations/Design/Fashion business. She is obsessed with keeping up with the times.

SAFFRON Edina's teenage daughter. She is the complete opposite of her mother. Living with her mother forces her to take on the mothering role.

PATSY In her forties. Edina's best friend. Magazine editor, but spends most of her time hanging around drinking and smoking fags and joints, and trying to get everybody else to do likewise.

BUBBLE Edina's secretary. In her twenties. There is no obvious reason for her employment except she has the right looks and is good at booking lunches.

Cast List

Edina · JENNIFER SAUNDERS

Patsy · JOANNA LUMLEY

Saffron · JULIA SAWALHA

Bubble · JANE HORROCKS

Jonny · NICKOLAS GRACE

Lou-Lou · LUCY BLAIR

scene one Edina's Office

Dream sequence: loud rap music is playing. Edina is sitting at her desk. Also in the office are two clothes designers, looking at large drawings and photos of models. Other office staff are walking in and out carrying clothes on hangers, flower arrangements and bottles of wine. The effect is one of people being busy-busy, but nothing is really happening.

Edina *(Drinking huge glass of water and eating a McDonald's.)* Everything is perfectly under control. It's going to be the most fabulous fashion event ever. Celebrities from all over the world – Jerry, Marie, Paloma. All the top French and Italian models, ten Yasmin Le Bons. Every designer in the whole world. It's going to be the most fabulous event ever.

Edina's secretary, Bubble, enters.

Bubble Everything is perfectly under control. It's going to be the most fabulous fashion event ever. Celebrities from all . . .

Edina We know that, darling.

Bubble I've booked every model in the world . . .

Edina I know, darling, but what about the party?

Bubble That is all completely under control. We've moved Stonehenge to a tent in Hyde Park.

Edina Did you get permission for that, darling?

Bubble They were very happy for us to use it, as long as it's back for the summer solstice. They realize how important the fashion industry is to this country.

Edina Exactly.

Bubble What are you going to wear to the party?

Edina I don't know.

Bubble What are you wearing at the moment, Edina?

Edina I'm not wearing anything, Bubble. I'm completely naked, I don't know why.

There is little reaction from Bubble.

Bubble I see.

Edina But I don't want to wear anything that isn't completely 'happening'. What is 'happening' at street level?

Bubble Shops and traffic.

Edina What are the kids into?

Bubble This is what the kids are into. This is what's 'happening'.

She opens the door and a male model walks in wearing a completely unfashionable-looking Seventies outfit, followed by a female model in similar gear. Jonny enters. He is a male designer.

Edina Jonny! How's it all going?

Jonny Terrific. Everything is going absolutely perfectly.

Edina looks down at her desk at copies of mags like ID, *and compilations of photo stills, of people dressed in Seventies gear. The pace becomes more manic and the shots weirder.*

Edina But I simply haven't got anything Seventies!

scene two **Edina's Bedroom**

Dream sequence: Edina is manically sorting through rows of clothes on hangers. She is close to hysteria. She is clutching some nail scissors and is close to tears. She begins hacking away at her clothes, cutting off collars, cutting into trousers. In a time-lapse sequence she is seen first chopping up, then crudely sewing up an outfit. Her daughter, Saffron, appears shaking her head disapprovingly.

Saffron You stupid, sad, old cow.

Edina Oh, shut up. I will look fabulous.

The camera cuts to Edina in front of her mirror. She is wearing the dreadful botched outfit, and is a pathetic sight.

Edina I can't go to the party. I'll have to kill myself.

She raises the scissors as if to stab herself.

Saffron You'll never get through all that flesh with those. *(Hands her a butcher's knife.)*

scene three Edina's Bedroom

Reality: Edina wakes up. She is strewn across her bed in her all-white bedroom. There is a half-drunk bottle of red wine by the bedside and an ashtray full of joint ends. The radio is playing rap music. She comes to, leans over and turns off the music.

Saffron *(From upstairs.)* Thank you!

Edina blows her a huge childish raspberry. It is obvious she has a terrible hang-over. She clutches at her chest.

Edina Panic attack! Panic attack!

She swigs back the remainder of the red wine and searches in vain for a joint in the ashtray. There is the sound of footsteps coming downstairs. They stop outside her door. Edina panics and hides the bottle and ashtray under her sheets.

Saffron *(Outside the door.)* It's nine-thirty and your car's been waiting for an hour.

The footsteps pass on downstairs. Edina retrieves the bottle and tries to rub the stain of spilled wine off her sheet. She gets up, staggers to the window and opens the curtains. The effect of sunlight blazing through the windows into the white room blinds her. She falls back in shock, grabs a pair of sunglasses and goes in to the bathroom.

scene four Edina's Bathroom

Edina has her head down and is shaking out her hair. Eventually she looks up into the mirror pulling her best face. She pulls off the sunglasses and her disappointment is obvious.

Edina Old, old, old. *(She inspects her face closely and tries pulling it into different positions.)* Joan Collins ... Kim Basinger ... Ivana Trump ... *(She lets her face drop.)* Barbara Bush.

scene five Edina's Kitchen

Saffron is sitting at the table reading a newspaper. In front of her are the empty wine bottles and left-over take-aways from Edina and Patsy's binge the night before. Edina enters struggling to appear bright, alive and healthy. Saffron watches her icily. Edina removes her tinted contact lenses, and it is obvious she cannot see a thing.

Edina *(Humming to herself.)* La, la la, la-la-la. *(She goes to fridge and gets bottle of Evian. She swigs it back and it suctions onto her face. She painfully pulls it off.)* Health, health, health.

She breezes around the kitchen opening cupboards and looking for something for breakfast. She opens the dishwasher, then the washing machine.

Saffron Washing machine.

Edina La-la, la-la! Absolutely right, sweetie. *(Opens freezer door.)* Just checking the contents. La, la, la. *(She does manic deep-breathing whilst slapping ice-cubes on her face.)*

Saffron *(Tapping the wine bottles pointedly with a pen.)* Feeling great, I expect, this morning, are you?

Edina *(Slamming freezer door.)* Fabulous. My god ... Patsy can put it away. *(She gives up looking for something to eat and staggers into a chair.)* Stop looking at me like that. What do I have to do to convince you that I've given up drinking? *(Pauses.)* I had *one* drink. I mean, for god's sake, are you accusing me?

Saffron Have you looked in the mirror this morning? Your eyebags are ruched.

Edina What are you eating?

Saffron Toast.

Edina What is that on the toast?

Saffron It's honey, mother.

Edina Oh, my god ... Oh, my god. Honey! That's not honey. Sweetie, that's my bloody royal jelly moisturizer. You are eating £300-worth of royal jelly that has been hand-squished from a bee's backside. And not just any old bee, but the bloody Gucci of bees. This is the stuff that Jackie Stallone would kill for. *(Edina scrapes it off the toast and rubs it onto her face.)* That's better. *(To Saffron.)* Make me a cup of coffee, darling. I've got a dreadful day ahead.

Saffron You know where it is – make it yourself.

Edina I don't know where it bloody is, do I?

Saffron Please don't swear.

Edina Sweetie ... darling, please fetch mama a cup of coffee. You're so clever, darling, you know where everything is, sweetie. I think it's so clever to know exactly where things are. I do think you're marvellous ...

Saffron Flattery won't turn me into your servant. The coffee is on the table in front of you ... Pick up a spoon ... Put coffee in cup ... Pour on boiling water.

Edina Scald hand ... Third-degree burns ... Screaming in agony. Do you really want that on your conscience, darling?

Saffron All right. *(She gets up to make the coffee.)*

Edina Not instant, darling. Grind some beans. That's not proper coffee ... that's just beans that have been cremated. I want them entire with lifeforce.

Saffron puts beans in the grinder.

Edina And don't make that face when you grind. I don't want to drink a cup full of your anger. Anyway, I shouldn't be drinking coffee . . . throw it all away. Throw all the coffee away. I don't want coffee. I just want some fennel . . . twig . . . tea.

Saffron sits down.

Edina Oh, god, look at the time. *(Grabbing the telephone she rings the office. Then she grabs Saffron and puts the phone to her ear.)* Sweetie, tell them I've left. Tell them it's traffic door-to-door, and I'm not well.

Saffron Hallo . . . my mother's sitting here in her dressing-gown . . .

Edina *(Grabs the phone, furious.)* Dressing-gown! Ha! Ha! She knows nothing about fashion. Now, Bubble, darling, I'm in a dreadful panic. I'm literally out the door when my bloody car turns up. I understand the traffic's awful. I'm desperately trying to keep a lid on things this end and I know you can manage that end. I'm frantic. I'm on my way . . . Chanting as we speak. Bye. *(She puts down phone. Saffron smirks. Edina notices.)* Oh . . . ha-ha! You're not a Buddhist . . . you wouldn't understand.

Saffron Mum, you did it for a week. Which, admittedly for you, is a record.

Edina Darling, it's not a fad. It's not like crystals. *(She starts a chant, but can't remember it.)*

Saffron Please stop.

Edina You wouldn't say that if you knew how much we owed to my chanting. A lot of things in this house wouldn't be here . . . This house wouldn't be here . . . I chanted for this gorgeous house. I chanted to be successful, to believe in myself. *(Chants.)* Please let me make some more money so that I can buy Saffron some more books and a car. *(Pauses.)* In Buddhist, obviously . . . not in English when I do it properly.

Saffron What is it . . . some sort of cosmic cash machine?

Edina Don't be cynical. Not today. Today I need a little support.

Saffron Why is today such a panic anyway? It's only a fashion show and you've had six months to prepare it. Why is everything always so hysterical? All you've got to do is play a bit of music, turn on the lights, get some people who've thrown up everything they've ever eaten and send them down a catwalk. Greater feats have been achieved in less time and with less fuss.

Edina You're not quite with it, are you, darling?

Saffron Major motion pictures are made, huge concerts are put on in stadiums, for god's sake. Five-hundred thousand troops were mobilized in the Gulf and a war fought and won in less time, and without everyone involved having a nervous breakdown and being sent flowers. It cannot be that difficult.

Edina But, darling, every troop didn't have to contain Yasmin Le Bon. The generals didn't require big hugs after every manoeuvre. And the whole operation didn't have to be coordinated to rap and Japanese *avant garde* pipe music. Because I think, if it had, the outcome might have been very different. Now, if you'll excuse me, I'm going to get dressed. *(She gets up, then sits down again, picks up the phone and dials.)* I forgot to ring Chukhani. He was going to channel a colour for me to wear today. Hallo, Chukhani? *(Pauses.)* Edina . . . *(Pauses again.)* Green . . . Thank you. *(Puts the phone down.)* Don't look at me like that, Saffy darling. There is more to it.

Saffron Of course, there is. The bill.

Edina He doesn't just pick any colour himself. It is channelled to him by an ancient spirit who understands perfectly my karma and relates it to who I was in a previous existence.

Saffron So, who were you then in your previous life? I suppose the Elizabeth Taylor of the Ming Dynasty. Face up to it – you're just a mad, fat, old cow.

ABSOLUTELY fab

Edina *(Gets up in rage.)* Will you stop saying 'fat'. I know you're only saying it to annoy me. Stop it! Stop it!

Saffron I'm saying it because it's true.

Edina Well, really . . . Oh, god . . . Oh, god.

She flies across the room and bangs some objects on the table in fury.)

Saffron What? What suddenly happened then?

Edina Why do you pick on everything I do? All I ask is for a couple of tiny little things to help me . . . tiny little pleasures . . . little crutches to help me get through life.

Saffron Get through? Mum, you've absolved yourself of responsibility. You live from self-induced crisis to self-induced crisis. Someone chooses what you wear. Someone does your brain. Someone tells you what to eat, and, three times a week, someone sticks a hose up your bum and flushes it all out of you.

Edina It's called colonic irrigation, darling, and it's not to be sniffed at.

Saffron Why can't you just go to the toilet like normal people?

Edina Is that what you really want me to be? Normal? Some boring, normal, old toilet-goer? 'Where's mummy?' 'She's on the toilet.' 'But I want to go somewhere exciting and meet interesting people.' 'She can't take you . . . she's on the toilet.' They say anybody can go to the toilet, they say . . .

Saffron They obviously haven't seen you drunk.

Edina Can I just say, bloody thank you so bloody much for giving me such a supportive start to a really rather important bloody day. A lot of daughters might have offered to come along and help me today. But no. You've probably got something rather exciting on Radio 4 to listen to, or some new exhibit of test-tubes at the Science Museum to visit. So, it doesn't matter. I shall go alone. *(She changes mood.)* There is a party afterwards, that I shall go alone to as well.

She gets up, stomps upstairs. Saffron sits impassively at the table. After a moment Edina slinks slowly back into the room, looking at Saffron with a pathetically sad expression on her face. Saffron doesn't look up. She knows what is coming.

Saffron No.

Edina Darling, please . . . angel . . . sweetheart . . . baby doll.

Saffron It's your drama – you act in it.

Edina reacts 'Oh, very clever'.

Saffron I won't be your accessory. 'What shall I wear? The daughter or the Dior?' 'Look at Edina, isn't she marvellous. I don't know how she does it, and she's got a family. How clever!'

Edina Time of the month, sweetie?

Saffron No.

Edina I just thought you looked as if you were retaining water, that's all. *(Pats Saffron's bum.)* I've got some marvellous pills upstairs, darling, if you're worried. Pee it all out overnight. *(Pauses.)* You're not seeing your father tonight, are you?

Saffron No. Go and get dressed.

Edina *(Goes to leave, but creeps back even more pathetically than before.)* Should I have surgery? Darling, look at mama.

Saffron Yes.

Edina leaves.

Saffron Get your mouth sewn up.

Edina Still here. I heard that.

scene six Hallway

Edina comes downstairs wearing a psychedelic Lacroix catsuit. She is on a mobile phone, carrying an armful of jackets.

Edina I pay you to interpret my dreams. Can't you at least try and find a hidden depth? *(Listens.)* Yes, well, I'm not willing to believe that I'm simply that obvious. And if you're a bloody psychic psychologist, how come I always have to call *you*? *(Puts phone down.)* Saff, I'm off! I won't see you later at the party because you don't love me enough.

Saffron comes into the hallway.

Saffron What time will you be home? *(Looks at outfit.)*

Edina It's Lacroix. It can't look that bad. A bit tight maybe. Anyway, they'll think 'Wow! It's a Lacroix!' So it's all right. I don't know what to wear over it . . . I can't find anything to go with it.

Saffron Maybe I could throw up on something for you. *(Edina puts on a jacket.)* Oh, it looks like someone already has.

Edina Yes, Jean Muir.

The doorbell rings. Edina pulls open the front door. Patsy is standing there.

Patsy Darling . . .

Edina Pats . . .

Patsy Your car's here . . . Thought I might scrounge a coffee.

Patsy walks round corner and reels back at sight of Saffron.

Edina Darling, I'm in a panic of a rush. Saff is here, though.

Patsy What *are* you wearing, Eddy?

Edina Lacroix. *(Indicates the name which is woven into the front.)*

Patsy It's fabulous.

Saffron Why doesn't Patsy go with you, mother?

Edina Yes, why don't you? We'll talk in the car. Bye, sweetie. *(She kisses Saffron.)* Goodbye, darling. Have a little hair cut . . . Have a little bob.

Saffron Don't be . . .

Edina What?

Saffron Don't be . . . late . . .

Edina blows her a kiss as she leaves.

Saffron . . . or drunk.

scene seven Inside the Jaguar

Patsy and Edina are slumped in the back of the Jaguar being driven. They both light cigarettes.

Edina Stop me drinking today, Patsy. Saff has threatened to leave home again.

Patsy Darling, you don't drink.

Edina I'm not a drinker, but you know what it's like. She's . . . such a pig. *(Picks up mobile phone from her bag.)* I'm just going to call in. *(She dials.)*

Patsy What will you drink?

Edina I will drink water, Patsy.

Patsy gives a blank stare.

Edina It's a mixer, Patsy. We have it with whisky.

Patsy I just can't imagine it.

Edina *(On phone.)* Bubble, it's me. At last, I'm in the car coming in. Things are still under control this end . . . How is it with you . . . ? Good. Models . . . ? Good. Lights . . . ? Good. Guest List . . . ? Well, just do your best. Bye.

Patsy I tried not drinking once. I heard myself talking all night and then, worse than that, next day I had total recall. It was terrifying.

Edina From now on, I will only drink when I am thirsty.

Patsy Can you do that on your own? Surely, there's somebody you could pay to help you.

Edina I don't know, Pats. I've considered colour healing. I mean, that helped when I had my energy crisis in my vegan period.

Patsy What did they do?

Edina Held up a purple card and told me to eat meat. It worked! Or I could get one of those earrings put in, and just turn it when I crave alcohol. Not that I do crave it. I just don't really have the desire not to drink. But if I can prove to her that I can stop, then she can see I'm not an alcoholic and I can go on drinking.

Patsy Don't get an earring, darling ... It's all guess work. I had one put in to help me lose weight, but every time I turned it I just pissed my pants.

Edina I shouldn't have left Bubble so much to do.

Patsy Are you going straight to the office?

Edina Yes.

Patsy *(In baby voice.)* Past Harvey Nichols?

Edina No, Pats.

Patsy Could we?

Edina Patsy! Look at me. I'm rushing.

Patsy It's just I want to change these earrings. *(Shows the ones she is wearing.)* They're not broken ... I've just gone off them.

Edina I haven't seen those before!

Patsy *(Pointing to Edina's jacket.)* I haven't seen this before. *(Pauses.)* And it's practically lunchtime.

Edina Look, we can do Harvey Nichols quickly now, pick up some lunch and take it to the office. I just think that would look better.

Patsy Whatever. But remember, darling, it's your company . . . You're the boss . . . You can do what you want. Don't let them pressure you!

Edina I'll ring them now, tell them to expect me. *(Picks up phone.)*

Patsy You'll kill yourself the way you work.

Edina Yes, I'll call them later. Will you come to the show later? Saffy's refused and I need support.

Patsy Of course, you do. And, of course, I will.

Edina Deserted by son and daughter.

Patsy Where is Serge?

Edina Pot-holing with his university. I don't want to talk about it.

Patsy I mean, I sometimes wonder what the point of having children is . . . if they're not there at your launches. Did you tell them how important it was to you, darling?

Edina Well I faxed the bloody Dean, the bollocky halls of residence and the buggery mountain rescue. What more can I do?

Patsy Nothing, and you shouldn't have to. My god, look at you. You've been a fantastic mother. You've let them ruin your figure. You stretched your stomach beyond recognition. You've got tits to your knees. And what for? For a pot-holer, for god's sake, who has worn nothing but a purple nylon tracksuit for the last two years. Cut the cord, darling. *(Pointing.)* Left here, if we're going to Harvey Nic's.

Edina *(To driver.)* Left!

Patsy We'll go to Joe's cafe on the way back ... You need a pasta. Then we're going shopping. I've seen things for you. Look, there's Yamishi's new shop. Did you see it? Gorgeous window. Huge swathe of white chiffon over a terracotta pot.

Edina What does he sell?

Patsy (*Thinks.*) White chiffon? Or maybe terracotta pots. Or both.

Edina I thought it was clothes.

Patsy You can get white T-shirts.

They both slump. Edina looks out of the window and nervously at her watch. Patsy produces a pregnancy tester kit from her bag, looks at it casually, then shakes it worriedly.

Patsy Can I use your phone?

scene eight Edina's Office

Bubble is sitting in Edina's office. The clock shows three o'clock. Through the glass doors there is much activity – people coming and going, phone calls being answered. Everything is very modern, run by very modern people.

scene nine Outside Edina's Offices

The Jaguar pulls up. Edina and Patsy get out. Edina talks over-loudly as she walks in.

Edina I would only use that car, Patsy, if someone else was coming with me. Otherwise, I definitely wouldn't have used it. I wouldn't drive around in that huge car, pouring out pollution, if I was on my own. But there were three people in that car, so it's all right.

Patsy Oh, shut up. No one can hear you.

Edina (*On mobile phone.*) Bubble, I'm coming through the door now.

scene ten Inside Edina's Offices

Edina and Patsy enter the office.

Edina Right, don't panic. I'm here. Let's get things moving. *(Enters main office.)* Right, what's to do? Bubble? Darling, I'm sorry I'm so late.

Bubble I think everything's just about done.

Patsy There you are, darling. I told you things would manage without you. *(Pours glass of wine and takes it to Edina.)*

Edina Lights . . . music . . . stage . . . press . . . tickets . . . models . . . designers?

Bubble All in place.

Edina Clothes?

The young male designer, Jonny, bursts furiously in, followed by a model wearing one of his creations, which is basically chain-mail. He is clutching other outfits.

Jonny Hack off my tits . . . I'm having a nervous breakdown. I am a sinew on a stick. I am a nerve end about to ping into insanity.

Edina Jonny, darling.

Jonny *(In tears.)* I have been exposed to the hideous face-lifts on shoulder pads. Those bitch-buyers from Bloomingdales have told me my creations aren't wearable. Unwearable? *(Indicates model.)* I am an artiste. These are my canvasses. I'm not some blind tart seamstress huddled over her fabric in the Bois de Boulogne. These are to be worshipped. Did they ask Da Vinci for washing instructions? Picasso for zips? I'm going to do what every good Buddhist should do. I'm going to set myself alight.

Edina You're a genius, don't be crazy. You are an artiste, a creator, an innovator. Your clothes are fabulous. *(Jonny, flattered, has now completely recovered.)* You just put in some zips on the left-hand side and a little tag with washing instructions.

Jonny Oh, all right. *(They kiss.)* You're so good for me. *(He turns to leave and is confronted by Patsy who is standing holding a lighted match, challenging his Buddhist conviction.)*

Edina *(Settling down.)* Right, Bubble. Did all the models turn up?

Bubble Yes, every single one . . .

Edina . . . and the . . . ?

Bubble Oh, except one.

Edina Except one. You're not going to tell me it's Yasmin Le Bon.

Bubble No . . .

Edina Thank . . .

Bubble No, sorry, yes. Yasmin Le Bon is ill.

Edina *(Nearly fainting.)* Oh, my buggery bollocks. Why the bloody hell didn't you tell me earlier?

Bubble Her husband just rang and said 'Simon *Le Bon*', which I thought was rather amusing.

Edina Amusing?

Bubble Yes, very modern of him to have taken his wife's name. Still, I phoned around and I think I may have found a replacement.

Edina Who?

Bubble Betty Boo! *(Edina reacts with horror.)* Some of the designers aren't happy, but I said you'd speak to them.

Edina Shit! This is all your fault, Patsy.

Patsy It's all fixable.

Edina *(To Bubble.)* How's the celebrity and VIP list looking?

Bubble Good. I think. But you know me . . . I don't know anybody.

Edina Just tell me about Joan Collins, Stephanie Powers, Paloma Picasso, Catherine Deneuve and Charlotte Rampling. Give me some names, Bubble.

Bubble So far?

Edina So far.

Bubble So far – Sinnita and Anne Robinson *definite*, and we are chasing Anneka Rice. Gave up on Norma Major.

Edina *(Gaining sanity through panic.)* Get me my phone book . . . Princess Di has to have . . .

Bubble Anne.

Edina . . . somebody to sit next to. You don't get Princess Di . . .

Bubble Anne.

Edina . . . to a major fashion event and sit her next to . . . *(Stops and looks at Bubble.)*

Bubble Princess Anne.

Edina *(Hopefully.)* As well as?

Bubble Instead of. Only. Possibly with daughter.

Edina *(Speechless.)* Why?

Bubble Well, there was a bit of a mix-up. I didn't make the call. But she's very game and a really nice person.

Edina I wouldn't care if she was Mother Bloody Theresa . . . It doesn't matter for our purposes. What we need is a Princess with a press following, and a designer dress on her back.

Patsy Not someone who looks like she runs up her own.

Bubble Her people *were* a bit cagey about which designer she favoured.

Patsy The only label she wears is 'drip dry'.

Edina Right. Let's take stock. We've got three hours.

Patsy Finish the Chablis and walk away from it, my love.

Edina Don't be silly, Pats, this is the bit I enjoy. Bubble, who's helping you today? I told you to get an assistant.

Bubble Yes, I have. She's a friend of mine. She knows a lot about the fashion biz. Very experienced. *(She calls.)* Lou-Lou!

Edina PR? PA?

Lou-Lou appears at the door, but can't get it open.

Bubble No, ex-model.

Lou-Lou is still trying to get the door open.

Patsy Re-inforcing my prejudice with every pathetic attempt.

Bubble Push! What's push in French? Pousse, Poussin.

Lou-Lou gets in and walks languidly to Bubble.

Bubble Did you find the toilet, this time?

Lou-Lou *(Shakes head slowly and talks with a French accent.)* I don't know.

Patsy Right, I'm off. Are we eating?

Edina Yes. What do you like French or Italian, or . . .

Patsy No. Nobody's eating that sort of food any more. But there's a fabulous new Japanese in Mayfair. Everything is raw. Anything that's got a pulse is lunch.

Edina Whatever.

Bubble The magazine called for you, Patsy. They need some decisions about this month's cover.

Patsy Oh, really. What can they need to know? It's the same every month . . . a model in makeup with a vacant look on her face. Anyway, I might look in at the office on my way home. See you later, Eddy. I've left the bottle.

Edina I need a clear head just for the next three hours.

Patsy Do you want some coke? *(Produces an envelope.)*

Edina No thank you, sweetie.

Patsy Save it for later, then. Good luck.

Edina Goodbye, Pats.

Patsy Have you got something I can pee into? I want to do another test before I go.

Edina *(Hands her a vase.)* Wash it, this time. Who were you with last night, anyway?

Patsy Oh, he was just a windscreen washer I picked up at some traffic lights. Bum's so tight he was bouncing off the walls. Goodbye, darling. *(Creepy mood change.)* You're a fabulous, wonderful individual . . . and remember that I know better than your daughter . . . and anything you do is all right by me . . . and I'm your best friend. Can I take your car?

Edina As long as he's back by six.

Lou-Lou *(As Patsy moves to the door.)* Push.

Patsy pulls open the door and exits.

Edina Right, get me a list of every record and PR company in the country, a copy of *Who's Who?* and the latest issue of *Hello!* magazine. Let's get celebritied up.

scene eleven Edina's Office

Five time-lapsed montage shots: Lou-Lou is asleep on the couch. Bubble is walking busily around the office.

1:

Edina is manically making phone calls, whilst flicking through Hello! *magazine.*

Edina We'll send a car for you . . . and fabulous curtains, by the way. And fabulous dress.

2:

Edina *(To Bubble.)* We'll make it a charity event. Children's charities and AIDS. Get on to Princess Anne's people and tell them everyone there will be mentally ill, and we'll sponsor her to wear a Vivienne Westwood. And make sure she realizes that if she doesn't those poor little children get nothing.

3:

Edina is desperately trying to resist the glass of wine in front of her. She sniffs it in desperation.

Edina Bubble, get four huge video screens. I want them down the side of the catwalk so we can flash up pictures of sad, but beautiful, children from round the world. Happy gay couples. And slogans like 'No Pollution', 'World Health', 'Fashion Cares'. Print up thousands of new invites on green paper and cab them round to everybody.

3A:

Edina selects photos of smiling children, seals, whales, trees, factories, gay people, disabled people, starving people.

4:

She dips her tongue in the wine.

Edina Bubble . . . Press Release. Free Champagne reception. Then get onto Moet and tell them it's charity. Ring Joan Collins . . . tell her it's free Champagne.

5:

Edina Bubble, let's get down to the event. I can't possibly wear this. Get me an item from each collection. I want to look up-to-the-minute ... and completely unbiased. And look at this, Bubble. *(She points to the undrunk glass of wine.)*

scene twelve Fashion Show Corridor

A small corridor, close to the catwalk entrance, is very crowded with models dashing off and on the catwalk. Designers are doing last-minute pinning, punctuated by kisses and hugs, and sips of Champagne. In the background there is music and applause. Edina is amongst the crowd, squashed against the wall. As various designers go by, she hugs each one and tells them their collection is a triumph and that the Japanese buyers love it. There are special hugs for Jonny, who is in tears, having a nervous breakdown. Two purple-coloured models come off the catwalk and squeeze past Edina. Most of the purple rubs off on her. She makes her way to the door and goes out.

scene thirteen Green Dressing Room

People are coming and going, drinking Champagne. There are many bouquets around, and half-naked models, smoking fags. Patsy is slumped on a sofa in the corner. Edina enters looking a disaster.

Edina Fabulous. It's absolutely fabulous out there. People are loving it. It's a huge success, Pats. Names ... names ... names queuing up to be seen with celebrities. All big designers ... Givenchy, Lagerfeld, St Laurent. English *Vogue*, French *Vogue*, American *Vogue*, Aby-bloody-ssinian *Vogue*. All the rich bitches from New York ... Huchenbuper, Hockwender, Vanderbilt, HuckenFuckenbergen, Rottweiler, Dachshund.

Patsy Whole row of skeletons with Jackie O hairdos.

Edina Selina Scott and Jeff Banks couldn't even get a ticket. I will go down in history as the woman who put Princess Anne in a Vivienne Westwood basque.

scene fourteen Edina's kitchen

It is very late. Saffron is sitting in her dressing-gown, reading. Every now and then, she looks out of the window expectantly.

scene fifteen Edina's Office

Late at night. The lights come on and Patsy and Edina enter. They are very drunk, but still drinking. Their clothes and makeup are a mess.

Patsy Let's go away.

Edina When?

Patsy Now. On holiday.

Edina I can't. I promised Saff I'd come home. Don't make me go on holiday. *(She crawls over the back of a sofa.)*

Patsy Darling, you need a holiday. How long is she going to be around for? She's been around forever.

Edina She's sixteen, Patsy.

Patsy Sixteen years you've had her. Sixteen years. Get rid of her.

Patsy Montserrat. I want to go to Montserrat.

Edina Look at me, Patsy. You're looking at a huge success.

Patsy I know.

Edina I've got fabulous kids who adore me. *(She starts to heave into tears. Patsy is unmoved.)* I'm sorry, but I just moved myself ... Where was I?

Patsy You were about to tell me about their bastard fathers ...

Edina Bastard fathers. I married two of the biggest shits in the world. I don't know why it went wrong with Justin ... We adored each other and then ...

Patsy He's gay.

Edina That wasn't the reason ...

Patsy *(Moving to sofa.)* Let's go on holiday.

Edina Look, Patsy. Maybe I should have some coffee. I don't want Saffy to know I've had a drink.

Patsy You're only saké drunk. It'll wear off.

Edina I think there may be some tea here, but no milk.

Patsy I'll go and get some milk. *(Gets up.)*

Edina No, don't. I don't really want tea. Where would you get milk from? What places sell milk?

Patsy Delicatessens.

Edina Oh! No. Don't bother. I don't want delicatessen milk. She'll never know.

Patsy She's not your mother.

Edina We got away with it then. My stupid bloody mother never noticed. My stupid bloody daughter won't . . .

Scene fades into a flashback. They are remembering their teens.

scene sixteen Flashback

It is 1968. Edina is staggering up a garden path in suburbia. Patsy and a couple of boys say goodbye. Edina takes deep breaths and goes into the house. She is completely stoned, trying desperately to act normal. Her mother appears.

Mother Hallo, Edina dear. Good concert? Why don't you come in and tell us about it? Your father and I are in the sitting room.

Edina I'm very tired actually.

Mother Come on.

Mother goes into the sitting room. Edina collapses. She gets up very slowly. A massive amount of concentration is required to follow her mother. Everything is swaying. Her mother's face is very close to her.

Mother Where was the concert, dear? Eel Pie Island again? Who was it? Anyone we should have heard of? The Beatles,

The Stones, The Rolling Who? You look a bit dizzy, dear, are you okay? Is that cider I can smell on your breath?

Mother's face comes very close to smell Edina's breath.

Flashback fades.

scene seventeen Outside Edina's House

Edina's car pulls up outside her house. Patsy gets out first, and goes to open Ed's door.

Patsy *(To Edina.)* She's not here, darling. *(The car door opens and Edina falls out, bottom-first onto the pavement.)*

Edina Help me, Patsy.

Saffron appears at front door. Patsy gets back into the car, and it drives off. Edina stands, shakily focussing on the door and tries to make her way to it.

Edina Sweetie, you needn't have waited up.

She staggers and falls into the window well beside the front door, bottom-first, so no danger of real injury.

scene eighteen Inside Edina's Kitchen

Edina's face appears outside window. She pulls herself up and flattens her inebriated face against the glass.

Edina Saffy, darling, let me in. *(Getting angrier.)* Saffy, sweetie, let me in. *(Shouting.)* Saffy, DARLING, LET ME IN.

scene nineteen Edina's Bedroom

Saffron is trying to put Edina to bed. Edina is running round the bed.

Edina Where's my joint box? Who's stolen my joint box?

(Eventually she collapses onto her knees.) Darling, Saffy, help me, now. Help mama, now.

scene twenty Edina's Kitchen

It is mid morning. The phone rings. Saffron answers it. Edina enters.

Saffron *(On the phone.)* Hang on a moment. *(To Edina, who is busy reading the instructions on the instant coffee jar.)* Mum, it's the Betty Ford clinic.

Edina *(Slightly surprised.)* Oh, yes. What do they want?

Saffron They say they're confirming the booking for four weeks from next Monday.

Edina *(Nods.)* I think it's the only way, darling. I know it's been difficult for you. So, I'm swallowing my pride and . . .

Saffron gives her a big hug. There is a little emotional moment.

Edina You've been very good to me, darling.

Saffron Well done.

Saffron exits. Edina picks up the phone.

Edina Thanks, Pats.

Cast List

Edina · JENNIFER SAUNDERS

Patsy · JOANNA LUMLEY

Saffron · JULIA SAWALHA

Bubble · JANE HORROCKS

Mother · JUNE WHITFIELD

Penny Caspar-Morse · ALEXANDRA BASTEDO

Justin · CHRISTOPHER MALCOLM

Georgy · ANTHONY ASBURY

`scene one` Edina's Bedroom

Edina is standing in front of mirror. She is desperately and rather tragically trying to squeeze her mass into a variety of outfits. She eventually finds a dress and, by compressing her bust manually, can zip it up.

Edina Yes ... Yes ... Be all right with a bit of jewellery.

She exits to the bathroom to the sound of a loud rip. In the bathroom the camera is at foot level, close-up on three pairs of bathroom scales. She stands on one.

Edina No ... No ... No ... *(She stands on another pair.)* No ... No ... No. *(We see the dress drop to the floor. Then she stands on the third pair.)* Not possible. *(She goes for a pee. We hear the flush. She returns and stands on the scales.)* No ... No ... There's not enough on my bones for that kind of weight. *(The earrings drop to the ground.)* But those are real gold. They must weigh more!

`scene two` The Kitchen

Saffron is eating breakfast in the kitchen, pain au chocolat and coffee. Edina enters in orange loose clothes, chanting.

Saffron Oh, dear!

Edina Morning, sweetie. I'm only wearing orange from now on – for religious purposes.

Saffron You've been getting dressed for three hours and you look like a bloated citrus fruit.

Edina It's a good healing colour. I'm getting rid of all my other clothes.

Saffron Is that the best you could come up with?

Edina *(Giving in.)* Darling, only this and the dreaded kaftan fitted. I say fitted – it was filled to capacity. Why? My whole wardrobe has developed stretchmarks. You wouldn't believe how much I weigh ...

Saffron I would.

Edina I know I don't look hugely overweight.

Saffron You do.

Edina But what I saw in the mirror shocked me. Barbara Bush with no clothes on.

Saffron Who did you expect?

Edina Marisa Berensen, of course.

Saffron Who?

Edina I have only ever seen Marisa Berensen . . . *(She thinks.)* . . . sometimes Cher.

Saffron *(Walks to cooker.)* Pre-knife? Do you want a cup of tea?

Edina Coffee, black. I shouldn't drink milk. Oh, god, why am I so fat?

Saffron You're not *so* fat.

Edina I am. Why?

Saffron Mum, you eat too much. You drink too much and you take no exercise.

Edina It's much more likely to be an allergy to something. A build up of toxins or a hormone imbalance. You know, darling, I have a very heavy aura. That's why animals love me.

Saffron They just see you as something to hibernate in. I take it you want a chocolate croissant, then.

Edina Pain au chocolat in this house, sweetie. No, I'll just nibble a corner of yours. *(She picks up the phone.)* Only one thing to be done. *(Dials.)* It's just the chocolate I have to avoid . . . I can eat the pastry. *(Puts phone to ear, nibbles croissant.)* Can I speak to Dr Jackson. It's Edina. *(Nibbles croissant.)*

Saffron *(Disapprovingly.)* Mum!

Edina Phillip! Eddy. Now, sweetie. Can I send someone round to pick up some more of those pills? *(Nibbles croissant.)* I want to lose a stone. *(Nibbles croissant.)* Two weeks ... Can't you just put them in an envelope and ...? Well, it must be a year since I had them last ... *(Nibbles croissant.)* They were just palpitations, for god's sake. Are you saying I can't have them? ... *(To Saffron.)* Well, what's the point of having a private doctor if they won't do what you want. *(Pathetically.)* Pleeeease ... I *want* them to kill me.

Doctor puts the phone down.

Edina Phillip! I can't believe this! He won't give them to me.

Saffron Good. You can't just take huge quantities of speed to lose weight.

Edina You can, sweetie. He treats royalty. *(Finishes croissant.)* Who wouldn't suffer a mild coronary for that degree of weight loss?

Saffron Mum, all you've got to do is eat less and take a bit of exercise.

Edina If it was that easy, darling, everyone would be doing it. Anyway, what do you mean? I do exercise.

Saffron You get out of bed. It ends there.

Edina I'll wait till Patsy gets here and then phone her doctor, and if I get no luck there I might go down to the Chinese clinic.

Saffron Here we go!

Edina The main trouble is not how much I eat, but what I eat. *(Crosses to the fridge-freezer and flings open the door.)* The fridge is filled with crap. I should only eat organic food, food with dirt all over it. I want all the food in this house thrown away. And I want just pure white and green organic foods, and rice noodle soup. Mmmmmm ... *(Licks finger.)* Delicious, isn't that from last night, sweetie? First, I should fast for a few days ... *(Reacting to Saffron staring at her.)* Darling, not the sort of fast you're thinking of. A special fast.

Saffron A sort of eating a lot sort of fast.

Edina Try and help me. Try!

Saffron What can I do? What can I say?

Edina Just try and be a little bit less western in your thinking. I mean, in Zen terms, darling, we are all just molecules. Ying and Yong. These are my molecules, those are your molecules. There is no difference between me and the table, me and a tree, me and Madonna, for god's sake!

Saffron Except you have a fatter bottom!

Edina Shut up!

Saffron Well, what do you want me to say? It doesn't matter to me that you haven't seen your navel in twenty-five years and that you can wear your stomach as a kilt. Tell me you're happy.

Edina How can I be happy with this great bulk hanging off my skeleton?

Saffron All right then, do something about it. But do something sensible.

Edina 'Sensible', sweetie. Can you not say that word.

Saffron You are not ill, you do not have a disease ...

Edina As far as I know ...

Saffron You are not menopausal.

Edina No! Still very much menstrual.

Saffron You have been tested for everything under the sun. You are not allergic to anything.

Edina Wrong! Jellyfish!

Saffron There's more of your blood sitting in test-tubes around the world than presently circulating in your veins. You have tried every fad diet, every fad drug that has ever existed. More money has been poured into your quest for 'Twiggyness' than goes in aid to most third-world nations . . . and somehow you're two stone overweight.

Edina One stone.

The entry phone buzzes.

Saffron Mum!

Edina For my height.

Saffron How tall . . .

Edina Six foot.

Patsy enters. She is coming down the stairs looking very pleased with herself, wearing a short skirt.

Patsy Morning, Eddy!

Edina Pats, stand there for a minute. I'm going to lift my shirt. I want an honest opinion. *(She lifts her shirt.)*

Patsy Surgery. Lipo, on the hips and stomach, bum lift, tit lift, lose a rib.

Edina looks horrified, puts shirt down. There is a young man standing next to Patsy. Edina is dreadfully embarrassed.

Edina Pats! My god!

Patsy This is Georgy. Say hallo, Georgy.

Georgy Hi! *(Winks at Edina.)*

Patsy Shall we have some coffee? Georgy?

Georgy Well, I have to be at the gym in a few minutes, so I better not. Thanks, anyway, ladies.

Patsy Girls, Georgy . . . we are girls. Goodbye then.

ABSOLUTELY fa

Patsy goes for a snog with Georgy.

Patsy Don't pump it too hard at the gym.

Georgy I'll see ya around.

Georgy exits.

Patsy *(To Edina.)* What do you think?

Edina He's nice, of a type, Pats.

Saffron A toilet-trained gorilla.

Patsy Nobody asked you.

Saffron You have nothing in common. You can't have anything to talk about.

Edina She doesn't want someone to talk to, do you, darling?

Patsy No, I've got you to talk to.

Edina Quite right. Nobody blinks an eye if an older man goes out with a young girl bimbo. But what's really sick is when a non-bimbo girl marries a really old man. That is sick.

Saffron What is this world you live in? What do you mean 'bimbo' and 'non-bimbo'?

Edina The real world, sweetie.

Patsy Eddy, you remember when I went out with Ferruzi.

Edina Are you listening, Saffy, this man was fifty-five.

Patsy The only thing that got him up in the night was his bladder. *(She has made a joke.)* Do you get it, Ed? He only got up to have a slash. Oh, forget it. Remind me not to tell that one when I'm sober.

Saffron Sober? Chance would be a fine thing.

Patsy turns her back on Saffron.

Patsy Right, Eddy. So, body crisis?

34

35

Edina Absolutely. Are you sure about surgery?

Patsy It's a viable option nowadays, darling. Everybody's doing it.

Edina My face?

Patsy Up to you.

Patsy hands Edina a hand mirror.

Edina I am a little Germaine Greerish.

Patsy God forbid.

Saffron I think she's great!

Edina She was *once* cool, darling, but Mr Gravity has been very unkind. Right, Pats, surgery on the face.

Saffron No.

Edina Darling, look at these wrinkles.

Saffron That's age. That's what happens.

Edina That is premature ageing, darling, therefore I can legitimately have it corrected.

Saffron You look fine.

Edina I could look better.

Patsy Time and money is all it takes. Look, Ed, best thing is . . . *(She gets out some magazines.)* . . . be scientific about it. Have a quick flick through these and find someone you'd like to look like.

The doorbell goes.

Saffron That'll be Dad.

Edina Oh, god, what's he doing here?

Saffron He's come to see *me*.

Saffron exits to get the door.

Edina I need inspiration, you're right. Maybe I should go out and buy some new clothes, but buy them two sizes too small. What's the recovery period on Liposuction?

Patsy Hours.

Saffron enters with Justin, her father.

Justin Hallo there.

Patsy Justin. *(Kisses him.)*

Justin *(To Edina.)* Hallo, sweetness.

Edina I didn't know you were coming.

Justin I thought you'd be at work. I've come to see my daughter. *(Cuddles Saffy.)*

Edina She's my daughter, too, you know.

Justin I'll never be able to forget that.

Edina Oliver's not with you, I hope.

Saffron Mum, stop it now.

Edina Darling, we are your parents having a civilized conversation. Butt out! *(To Justin.)* How are things with Oliver?

Justin They're good.

Edina Oh, good . . .

Patsy Steady, Eddy.

Edina But how could you have chosen to live with an evil, vicious, ugly little pot-bellied dwarf is beyond me.

Justin *(To Saffron.)* We were happy for a time, you know.

Edina And then you turn up here, with not so much as a present for me.

Saffron Don't, Dad, not this time.

36

Edina Here I am coping on my own. Running a business, bringing up your daughter, coping on my own.

Justin *(To Edina.)* Okay, in the shop there's a lovely little two-hundred-year-old Indian turban box, silver inlaid, and beautiful hand-painted scenes on the lid.

Edina How much?

Justin Worth about a thousand pounds.

Saffy sickened.

Edina *(Baby-voice.)* Tank you!

Patsy looks miffed.

Justin *(To Patsy.)* Oh, and I have a lovely eighteenth-century walnut table with turned legs that would be heavenly in your dining room, Patsy.

Patsy Fank you, Justin. *(To Edina.)* Come on. Let's go, Ed. The car's outside.

Saffron *(To Justin, double sickened.)* Stop compensating her. It's been ten years.

Edina Bye, darling.

Saffron Driving in?

Edina Yes? What do you think I should do—fly? *(Realizing that might not be a bad idea.)*

Saffron I just find it strange. I just don't understand how someone can have been into absolutely everything for the past twenty years, not one trend passed you by and yet somehow you've conveniently dodged ever having to take exercise. That craze, that fad was missed by a mile.

Edina Stop showing off in front of your father. Can I explain, darling? Justin, help me here. In the Sixties we were too stoned, and in the Seventies we had platform shoes, and in the Eighties

... I can't remember what happened in the Eighties. *(Can't think of an excuse.)*

Justin Too many brain cells died in the Sixties.

Edina What was it?

Justin Punk.

Edina We were too busy sticking safety pins through our noses.

Saffron You were too old to be a punk, weren't you, Mum?

Edina Darling, I was a punk.

Saffron I know. *(Takes a while for this to sink in.)*

Patsy Don't let her torture you, Eddy. She's the one that ruined your figure in the first place, that turned you into this ... potato ... we see before us.

Justin I think she looks divine. I used to like you when you were more ... er ... cuddly ...

Patsy I'm going to throw up.

Justin I mean tough.

Patsy Let's go.

Edina *(Insulted beyond belief.)* We'll go on public transport, Pats.

Patsy What? I haven't got anything to wear on public transport.

Edina I won't have my daughter thinking she's so bloody marvellous because she uses public bloody transport. *(She goes up close to Saffy.)* Anybody can use public bloody transport, darling.

Saffron I know, that's the point.

Edina *(Going up the stairs.)* I've got the map book thing, Patsy. London street map book thing.

scene three Exterior of Edina's Office

Taxi pulls up. Edina and Patsy get out.

Patsy *(Shouting.)* On account.

Edina I mean, it is public and it is transport.

Patsy Of course it is. You don't have to travel on rat-infested sewer trains to be using public transport.

Edina That would be ridiculous.

scene four Inside Edina's Office

Bubble is sitting reading a magazine. As Edina and Patsy enter she starts shuffling paper and dusting, throwing faxes in the bin, etc.

Edina I'm here. Don't panic. Everything under control?

Bubble Yes, everything is perfectly under control.

Edina Sorry to be so long, sweetie. Had to do a spot of clothes shopping along the way.

Edina sits at her desk. Patsy sits on sofa with bottle of Beaujolais and cigarette.

Edina Anything important come in I should know about?

Bubble A few of the . . . oh, what d'you call 'ems came through.

Edina What?

Bubble The paper that comes out.

Edina What? What paper?

Bubble Very important, urgent, paper.

Edina What? Tell me.

Bubble The paper that comes out of the answer machine.

Edina Fax?

Bubble Messages, letters, the lot. It comes and comes. Anyway them. There's a couple of them. I've copied them onto my pad.

Edina Let's have a look. *(Takes pad.)* One. We are being saved by English Heritage.

Bubble Are we?

Edina Yes. Here. Saved?

Bubble No. *(Laughs.)* Sued!

Edina Only four letters out. Why sued?

Bubble That last fashion shoot you organized ... apparently they moved a couple of rocks or something.

Patsy Moved a couple of old rocks.

Edina It was Stonehenge, Pats.

Patsy So? They should be glad of the publicity.

Edina Exactly. Send it to the lawyers. And two ... Penny called from LA. Penny? Penny who?

Bubble It'll come to me. It's only urgentish. She's coming over, I think in a week or two, and wanted to talk about a shop or something. Wants to sell you things or something.

Edina My shop, Bubble, remember. I'm going to open a shop. I miss not having a shop, Pats.

Patsy What are you going to sell?

Edina You know, just gorgeous things.

Patsy Ooooooh, lovely.

Edina Just gorgeous, lovely, tasteful, beautiful, stylish ...

Patsy Expensive ...

Edina Obviously, Anoushka Hempelly presenty things.

Patsy Chocolates.

Edina Garden implements. *(She has been looking through a magazine.)* I can't find anyone I really want to look like, Pats. Who's that?

Patsy Ivana Trump?

Edina Not bad.

Bubble God, do you think so? *(Picks up the picture.)* Looks like the classic bimbo to me. Look at that terrible blonde hair piled on top of her head, false tan, she's far too thin, always pouting, absolutely no character, skirts too short. I mean, it's a pathetic older woman struggling to look twenty-five.

The atmosphere has grown tenser and tenser. As Bubble goes on, it is clear Patsy is taking it personally. Bubble stops, realizing she has been describing Patsy.

Bubble Sorry.

Patsy I think she's tremendous.

Edina You're very thin, Bubble.

Patsy Emaciated . . . like her brain.

Bubble I know, it's awful. I can eat as much as I like and I just don't get fatter. I cannot put on weight.

Edina How dreadful!

Bubble I know. I wish I was more curvy. I wish I had breasts like yours.

Edina No, you don't.

Bubble Yes, I do.

Edina No, you don't.

Bubble I do. Great big large pendulous breasts. I'd like to fill a bra.

Edina *(Getting aggressive.)* No, you don't. Don't say you do, you don't. You have no concept of what it's like. You think because you look better with a couple of oranges stuffed in your cups you know what it's like. Well, you don't. It's hell.

Bubble I don't have to wear a bra. *(Pause.)* I just stuff the oranges down my vest.

Edina Now listen here, you bookmark. You know I only employ you because you make me look good, don't you?

Bubble *(Suddenly remembering.)* Penny Caspar-Morse. That's who's coming over.

Edina staggers upon hearing that name and collapses under her desk.

scene five Edina's Bedroom. Later

Bubble, Patsy, Saffron and Justin are gathered around Edina's bedside. She is delirious, slipping in and out of consciousness, muttering 'must lose weight' and 'Penny Caspar is coming and I'm fat'.

Edina *(Repeating deliriously.)* Penny Caspar's coming and I'm fat.

Saffron *(Bewildered.)* Who is Penny Caspar?

scene six Flashback to the Sixties

Very trendy brilliant white gallery, full of trendy, beautiful people, psychedelia and magazine covers featuring Penny Caspar 'the stick'. Everybody is hovering around Penny adoringly. Edina is with a man who leaves her and is soon seen snogging with Penny. Penny starts to taunt Edina and the group around her begins to laugh.

Penny *(Indicating Edina to her friends, and taunting Edina.)* Hey, who's that? Pat Ast? *(Pauses.)* Hey, there's the girl that gives the word 'hippy' a whole new meaning. *(To Edina.)* Move over Mama Cass. Move out the way, sweetie, you're blocking my light. Is it an eclipse? Oh no, Edina's in the room. We could cancel Woodstock everybody. They can play on Edina's behind!

scene seven Edina's Bedroom

Edina is having a fit on the bed.

Bubble What's she doing?

Saffron What pills did you give her, Patsy?

Patsy *(Looking guilty.)* Just some tranquillizers. Don't question me.

Justin I think she's sleep-jogging. You know, she did this for about three weeks before we got married. She was really anxious about her weight. She wanted to get married in hot-pants.

Edina doing convulsive jumps in bed.

Bubble Did she?

Justin No, knickerbockers.

Patsy Poor old, fat old thing. Look at her. Like a beached whale in designer sheets. It can't have been easy for her, growing up in our generation. The era of 'The Shrimp' and 'The Twig'. Penny Caspar was called 'The Stick'. What hope did *she* have?

Bubble What did they call her?

Patsy Eddy was called 'The Shredder' because she used to eat huge amounts of tissues.

Justin Whole toilet rolls.

Saffron Oh, god. But it's pathetic. I mean she's not even fat.

Bubble And I'm Dolly Parton.

Patsy You're right. She is desperately unhappy. We've got to help her. I'm gonna do something. I'm not gonna let her down. I'm gonna get her damned well thin so she can face that damned bitch, Penny Caspar, with some dignity. Damn it! I mean she means a lot to all of us.

Bubble looks doubtful.

Patsy Well, anyway, she's been a damned good friend to me. We've got to help her. She's got no willpower. She's helpless. We've been through a lot together and I'm gonna be there for her. *(Sits down beside Eddy.)* Wake up, Eddy. *(Slaps her face.)* Eddy, wake up. Damn you. It will be all right. You will damned well be thin, you will damned well damned be damned thin. *(Clutches Edina's hand dramatically.)* Oh, god, Eddy don't sleep. *(To Saffron.)* We may have to pump her out again.

scene eight **Bathroom**

Edina is in a tracksuit, obviously dressed for a work-out. Patsy, in usual gear, is seated on side of bath. Georgy is dressed in full work-out gym kit.

Georgy *(To Edina.)* Okay, let's start with those abdominals. Let's see whether we can get that stomach flat. Okay.

Edina Tomboyish!

Patsy Go for it, Eddy. *(She lights cigarette.)*

Edina and Georgy lie down on their backs on the floor.

Georgy Okay, let's start with ten.

Edina I do them as well? Yeah, yeah.

Georgy Yeah, come on up. Okay. Now, I don't want to see a big movement, just enough to get your head and your shoulders off the mat.

Patsy Go for it, sweetie. *(Flicking through magazine.)*

Georgy Okay, here we go. *(He lifts his head and shoulders. Edina remains still.)* And one ... And one ... Feel those muscles pull in.

There is no movement whatsoever from Eddy.

Edina Show me that again. The . . .

Georgy *(Demonstrates.)* Just scrunch up like that. Just try and get your head and shoulders off the mat there.

Edina *(Not moving a muscle.)* No.

Georgy Your head?

No movement from Eddy.

Edina I can move my eyes.

Patsy Well done, sweetie.

Georgy That's good. That's good. Yeah. It's a muscle.

Edina *(Patting her stomach.)* I feel it . . . here.

scene nine A Street in Edina's Neighbourhood

Edina is out jogging. She is having trouble keeping her headphones on and is struggling to find the right track.

scene ten Edina's Kitchen

Mother and Saffron are in the kitchen making tartlets. Edina jogs in down the stairs. She is breathless.

Saffron How far did you get?

Edina can't catch her breath. Her face is very red. Indicates a circuit.

Saffron You did a circuit?

Mother Round the living room, dear?

Edina No, I went across Mead Avenue, Elgin Road, Moore Place, right round the crescent, past the traffic lights, then home.

Saffron End of the road and back.

Edina *(Reluctantly.)* Yes.

Saffron How long have you got left?

Edina Four days.

Mother Shouldn't eat so much, little piggy. *(She snorts.)*

Edina I'm not eating anything. Nothing. I'm living on air and mung beans.

Mother You've got your grandmother's hips.

Edina Thanks to you. Thanks to all the chips and lard, and potatoes, and white bread, and suet pudding with treacle you forced me to eat as a child. Endless cups of sugary tea and . . .

Mother Mr Whippy.

Edina And biscuits, and puddings, and meat fried in six inches of animal fat. Thanks to that.

Mother *(To Saffy.)* Before we got the deep-freeze.

Edina Even after it was the same food . . . just colder. But the real problem began with the fact that I wasn't even breastfed.

Mother Don't be ridiculous. It wasn't done in those days. *(To Saffy.)* Imagine me having that clamped to my breast. *(Indicating Edina.)*

Edina Anyway, I want better for Saffy. I don't want her ending up looking like me with all my very marvellously complicated hang-ups. At least, she was breastfed.

Saffron Was I? By whom? You told me your milk dried up, your tubes blocked, and your nipples dropped off.

Edina Yes, they did.

Saffron Well? Who was I breastfed by? Not one of the many saggy-titted hippies who lived with us at the time, I hope.

46 | 47

Edina It was a commune, that was the point. Anyway, you got a good start.

Silence.

Edina You're all right, aren't you?

Silence.

Edina You're all right, aren't you?

Saffron How many? Just tell me how many.

Edina Well, you're not fat like me. What you don't realize is that inside, inside of me there is a thin person just screaming to get out.

Mother Just the one, dear?

scene eleven Inside Edina's Office

Patsy and Edina are trying to get Edina into some trousers. Bubble enters.

Bubble Leggings?

Patsy Slacks.

Bubble Oh, dear.

Edina What am I going to do?

Patsy How comfortable are you?

Edina On a scale of what?

Patsy Childbirth.

Edina Well, I'd say a twelve-pound baby, no anaesthetic and forceps. I could live with it. What do they look like?

Patsy A zeppelin in a condom. You'll have to try something else.

Bubble You could get your jaw wired up.

Edina I tried that years ago. It lasted two days. My will to speak was too strong.

Patsy Well we're still all right. There's still time to get to the clinic and have Lipo as a last resort.

Edina So, if Penny gets here on . . .

Edina and Bubble both speak together.

Edina Tuesday.

Bubble Tomorrow.

Edina That gives me time. I can have lost another few pounds before . . .

Edina and Bubble together.

Edina Tuesday.

Bubble Tomorrow.

Edina What?

Bubble Tomorrow. *(Pause.)* Evening.

Edina Why are you saying that?

Bubble Because it's true. She rang.

Edina *(Panic attack.)* Oh, no . . . oh, no . . . oh, no . . .

Patsy I'm ringing the clinic. *(Speaks into phone.)* Emergency Liposuction. *(Hands the phone to Edina.)* Get collagen lips done, too. I want to know how painful it is.

scene twelve **Edina's Bedroom**
Edina is tossing and turning in her sleep obviously having a nightmare.

scene thirteen **Dream Sequence**
Edina is lying in a very dark, weird medical-type room. A surgeon, dressed in blood-spattered overalls, is holding a Lipo sucker.

Surgeon How small do you want to be?

Edina *(Holding up a pair of dolly trousers.)* This small.

She is now lying on operating table. It's very dark, strange lights, not real. We see the surgeon plunge in the sucker to Edina's leg. She is screaming.

Surgeon Oh, no. *(Panicking.)* Oh, no.

There is the noise of two lumps being sucked out of Edina's body.

Surgeon The kidneys! Oh, no. It's out of control. I can't stop it. Oh no, come back.

Horrific scene as the whole of Edina's insides are sucked out and her body is left like a deflated blow-up doll. Edina is screaming.

Surgeon Lips, madam?

The surgeon has a huge hypodermic syringe and pumps a substance into her lips. They grow bigger and bigger and bigger and look like they will explode!

Edina No more . . . No more . . .

scene fourteen Edina's Bedroom

Edina wakes up. It is morning. She is happy to find her body intact. She feels her lips.

Edina Oh, my body. I love you . . . my body. Oh, god. Oh, god. *(She reaches for the telephone, and dials.)* Pats? . . . *(Pauses.)* Well, is she there? Who are you? Well what does she look like? Well, turn her over and ask her name. Oh, Pats, it is you! Listen, Pats. Darling, I can't go through with it. I can't . . . No. Oh, all right.

scene fifteen Edina's Kitchen. Evening

Edina is trying to look thin. Mother, Saffy, Justin and Bubble are all waiting.

Edina *(To Saffron.)* Is it all right? *(Indicating.)* Thin ankles. *(To the others.)* You lot, don't just sit there. Remember when she comes, stand up straight, mill around me. Make a wall, here.

Justin You look great.

Saffron Shut up, Dad.

Edina Just keep it busy enough so she never gets a clear view. And all look happy . . . and you love me . . . We're still really great friends, Justin, and we touch a lot.

Justin If you say so. *(Very confused.)*

Patsy comes downstairs.

Patsy Okay. Okay. Okay. She's here. *(Goes to Edina who is sinking.)* Eddy. Great news.

Edina *(Thinks.)* She's fat! *(Throws up arms in joy.)*

Patsy No, no, no. Better.

Edina She's dead.

Patsy No. She's *blind!!* Ha, ha.

Edina She's blind? She's blind. Oh, hurrah, hurrah, bloody buggery hurrah. She's bloody blind.

Penny *(Calling from upstairs.)* Patsy, are you there?

Patsy Coming, Penny.

Patsy fetches her down. She is very LA looking. She has bandaged eyes and dark glasses on top. As she comes down Bubble is trying to mill in front of Edina — she hasn't understood.

Penny Patsy, is Eddy here?

Patsy Just here.

Edina Penny! You're blind.

Penny It's a retina operation. I had it in LA. They said I would be okay by now, but I guess not. C'est la vie.

Patsy is behind Penny miming to Edina that she has had an eye job and it hasn't healed. Also pointing out Penny's obviously collagen lips, tit implants and bum lift.

Penny Where are you, Edwina? *(Holds out her hand.)*

Edina *(Doesn't know what to do.)* Just here. It's Edina.

She grabs Bubble and pushes her towards Penny who embraces her.

Penny Wow! You've lost weight.

Edina *(Speaking from behind Bubble.)* Well, I keep busy. Poor you, though.

Patsy Poor you.

Edina You look well. How do you do it?

Penny Oh, you know.

Patsy Yes, I do.

Saffron *(Very annoyed by the goings on.)* Are you going to introduce everybody else?

Penny Who's this that I hear?

Edina My gorgeous and darling daughter Saffron. Say hallo to Penny.

Saffron *(Shakes her head.)* And my ... *(She is about to introduce Justin.)*

Edina ... my new man in my life ... Michael is here. But he has to go ... Just shake hands then go, Michael.

Justin *(Very, very confused. Saffron very angry.)* Oh, okay. Goodbye.

Edina Goodbye you gorgeous, handsome, rich thing.

Penny Where is your son, Serge?

Edina Oh, you just missed him. Did you see him on his way out? Oh no, of course not.

Saffron leaves with Justin.

Edina Sit down and have a drink, Pen.

Penny moves towards a chair and touches Mother.

Penny Who's this?

Mother is confused. Doesn't know who she is supposed to be. Edina mouths 'it's you', 'it's you'.

Mother *(Scottish accent.)* It's only me, dear.

Edina It's my mother.

Penny Hallo.

Mother Hallo.

Mother mouths that she is going. Edina mouths that she can talk if she wants to.

Edina Talk, Mother.

Mother I'll leave you to it. Goodbye. Bye, Patsy. *(Puts hand to mouth and whispers to Edina.)* It is Patsy, isn't it?

Mother and Bubble both exit.

Patsy Now, Pen. Tell us all. You're selling things now.

Penny I have a couple of shops in LA. One on Sunset that sells New Mexicana and I heard Edina was opening a shop.

Edina As a sideline. For fun. So, ya want me to buy a few of your little things?

Patsy What is New Mexicana?

Edina It's all those cheap little things that Indians make. First you take the country and then sell off the tomahawks. Scalp for scalp, eh Pats!

Patsy I never saw this as your type of thing, Pen. I mean selling crap with zig-zags on it. What happened?

Penny I want you to know I'm coping with this.

Edina What happened to that rich producer you married after Trevor came back to England?

Penny We had a mutual, contractual, consenting partition, type of thing.

Edina Did he dump you, too, darling? Well, what a shame.

Patsy Steady, Eddy.

Edina You took from me the only man I ever really loved. You were a spiteful bitch, Penny Caspar . . .

Penny Morse. Penny Caspar-Morse now.

Edina And now you come back trying to sell me some horrid little bits of tat for my shop. *My* shop. Well, what a come down. Yes, I'm successful, happy, got a wonderful family, friends.

She moves very close to Penny, grabbing her arm as she speaks.

Penny I want you to know I'm no longer coping with this.

Edina I don't have to resort to the plastic surgeon to keep myself together. I've got my own . . .

They are both standing now. Penny has grabbed Edina. Patsy is trying to warn Edina 'no, get away'.

Edina . . . fantastic bone structure. I'm thin and gorgeous.

Penny, furious, has got Edina in her clutches.

Penny (*Triumphantly.*) Thin?

Freeze frame on Edina's horror.

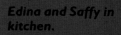

Edina and Saffy in kitchen.

'**G**ood morning, sweetie.' Edina looking gorgeous, Saffy not so.

'**D**ecisions, decisions!' Eddy and Patsy looking great.

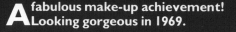

'**A** zeppelin in a condom.' Pats helps Eddy to look fabulous.

'**E**mergency liposuction.' Eddy needs a lot of help.

'But this is Spain, sweetie.' Gorgeous but lost.

'Straw Dogs?' No, it's Patsy and Eddy looking great in France.

'Ou est mes moutons?'

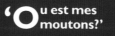

In wine cellar.

After a hard day's filming, Joanna and Jennifer find time to relax and pose for a photo.

Looking gorgeous, but should she have surgery?

france

Cast List

Edina · JENNIFER SAUNDERS

Patsy · JOANNA LUMLEY

Saffron · JULIA SAWALHA

Bubble · JANE HORROCKS

Mother · JUNE WHITFIELD

Customs Officer · GEOFF McGIVERN

Air Hostess · JULIETTE MOLE

Edina's Bedroom

Edina is packing. Bubble is on the bed, squashing clothes etc., into large expanding suitcase.

Edina I'll be gone the whole week, Bubble. I'm counting on you to cope. There's only one thing you have to concentrate on and that's the refurbishment of Bettina's apartment. I promised her it would be finished this week. I never realized she would be so difficult about it. When she said 'Third World Chic', I hoped she'd stick to it. It took me hours to get hold of fly-blown mud hessian for her kitchen walls. There's a nomadic tribe in the North African desert that will be travelling very light this winter, thanks to Bettina. Remember to stamp 'Greenpeace'-approved on the wood for her kitchen surfaces when it arrives. And if the silk for her cushions doesn't arrive tomorrow, fax Calcutta and tell them to weave faster. Poor Bettina! *(Goes into bathroom and starts to scoop cosmetics into bag. Looks into mirror and pulls a French face. Tries out some French. Reads out labels on her toiletries. 'Jeunnesse des mains'. 'Base hydratante'. 'C'est la vie'. Is very impressed by her own French accent. Goes back to bedroom. She is searching for something.)* I'll try and call on my mobile, but I'm not sure if it will work from France.

Bubble Even if it does I'm not sure I'd understand what you were saying.

Edina *(Confused.)* You do speak French, don't ya? Darling, everybody speaks French. *(Pause.)* Someone has been stealing from me.

Bubble Whereabouts is it you're going?

Edina A friend of Patsy's is lending us a gorgeous villa in the middle of nowhere, just outside St Tropez . . . Provence. En Provence.

Bubble Oh! So what shall I do in an emergency? Shall I have the address in case I need to . . .

Edina On no account are you to step foot in mainland Europe during the next week.

Bubble But . . .

Edina I will ring you.

Bubble But . . .

Edina You bring that suitcase, angel. I'll take this one. *(Picks up hand-luggage)*. I'm furious.

scene two Hallway

Edina and Bubble come downstairs. Edina is still searching. The case is so heavy it pulls Bubble down the stairs as they go down.

Edina Be careful of that case. *(Shouts.)* Saffy! Saff! *(Goes down to the kitchen.)*

scene three Edina's Kitchen

Edina and Bubble come down the stairs. Saffron and Mother are there.

Edina Saffy.

Mother Morning, dear.

Edina Oh, god! *(Looks at Mother.)* What are you doing here?

Mother I'm coming to stay, dear. While you are away. To keep Saffron company.

Edina You're not. Is she, sweetie?

Saffron I don't mind.

Edina Saffy doesn't want you to stay. Do you, darling? She wants a bit of freedom. Doesn't need you cramping her style. Wants to have parties, with boys and friends, play loud music and . . .

Bubble Have orgies.

Edina Yes, and smash the place up and crash out on the floor.

Bubble In a pool of sick.

Saffron I don't.

Edina Well, why bloody not? Just try it once.

Mother You're not like your mother in that respect, are you, Saffron? She spent most of her teenage years sitting on a large beanbag, cigarette in one hand, joss stick in the other, and with a large-lipped youth suctioned on to her face.

Edina Come here, Saffy, darling. Pats will be here in a moment.

Mother Shall I make some tea? Nice cuppa tea? Where would one find tea-bags?

Edina We don't have tea-bags. We have tea. *(Points.)* Saffy, don't wander away. Something has been stolen from my room.

Saffron What?

Edina A certain little something precious to me.

Bubble Have you seen this pot?

Edina *(Shocked.)* Where? Where have you seen it? Tell me.

Mother Sort of space-age teapot, isn't it, dear? A teapot to boldly go where no teapot has been before. To seek out new life forms.

Saffron I hid your stash.

Edina Where?

Saffron Down the toilet.

Mother Now, what might one use to put the tea into the pot with?

Edina A spoon . . . a bloody buggery teaspoon.

Mother Oh. *(Winks at Bubble.)* A bloody buggery teaspoon. That sounds rather clever. And where does one fill the kettle, from the bloody marvellous tap I suppose?

Edina No, the filter. *(In fury Edina grabs the kettle and fills it, ranting as she does so.)* God, why did you come round? Such endless bloody fuss! This is my house. This is where I do what I want. Why can't people let me get on with it? Busted by my own bloody daughter. *(Turns on Saffron.)* What am I supposed to do now?

Saffron What were you planning to do? Slide it in the lining of your handbag, or insert it in some orifice for some dog to sniff at? I can't believe you were thinking of taking it with you. I mean, I don't mind if you have the odd joint at home, in your bedroom.

Edina Darling, thank you. How kind! It was for personal use. You are allowed to have it for personal use.

Saffron Mum, they would send you to prison.

Edina Not somebody like me, sweetie . . . not any more.

Saffron Pathetic.

Mother This filtered water boils very quickly.

Bubble That's because there's less of it.

Saffron *(To Edina.)* They are illegal drugs. You use them like most people have after-dinner mints . . . to round off a meal. Either you sniff something to make you speedy or smoke a little something to make you jellybrained. Either way you end up more boring than you can imagine.

Edina That's rich coming from someone who lives their life at a level of boredom that would make a battery chicken think of taking up an evening class.

Saffron Mum, you are supporting a criminal, corrupt, evil system.

Mother Is she insisting on voting Labour again, dear?

Saffron You are no different to a junkie on the street, to a

58
59

dealer. As long as people like you go on doing it, giving it a hint of respectability, the evil will continue. Governments will be undermined, countries kept poor, children corrupted individuals will be killed, intimidated and tortured.

Edina I think you've overdosed on John Craven's *Newsround* again, darling.

There is the sound of car horn.

Mother I'll go.

scene four Hallway

Patsy enters, wearing St Tropez gear. Mother enters from kitchen.

Mother Patricia!

Patsy Hallo.

Shakes hands. Mother holds her hand and won't let go.

Mother Still no ring on that finger? No husband?

Patsy No one special. *(Shouts.)* Eddy!

Mother *(Sympathetic.)* Aaah! And you were always the one with the boys. Seems strange to me that Edina should have been married twice, and you a spinster.

Bubble *(Entering.)* Oh, I don't know.

Mother Still blonde, then?

Patsy Yes.

Mother Still managing to keep that up?

Patsy Yes. Is Eddy here?

Eddy and Saffron enter.

Mother Here they are. Lovely old Patsy is here, dear.

Patsy Come on, Eddy.

Mother Here's Patsy, Saffy. Here's Aunty Patsy, Saffy.

Patsy I'll wait in the car.

Mother Goodbye, dear.

Kisses her, fiddles with Patsy's hair as mothers do.

Saffron Goodbye, Aunty Patsy.

Patsy Come on, Eddy. *(Exits.)*

Edina Bye, Mum.

Mother Bye, dearest. Look after yourself. Got everything? Passport? Tickets? Etc?

Edina Yes. *(Goes to Saffron.)* Bye. *(They hug coldly.)* Have some parties. Have some boys round.

Saffron Be careful. Passport, tickets, condoms?

Edina *(To Bubble.)* Just remember one thing. Cancel aromatherapy, psychotherapy, and reflexology, osteopath, homeopath, naturopath, crystal reading, shiatsu, organic hairdresser . . . And see if I can be rebirthed the following Thursday afternoon.

Bubble Right. *(Crosses her fingers at Edina.)*

Edina Bye. *(Exits.)*

Mother *(To Saffron.)* You don't mind if I stay, do you?

Bubble No, not at all. Feel at home.

Saffron No, not at all.

Bubble Oh, sorry.

Mother Shouldn't you be getting to the office?

Bubble looks at Saffy.

Saffron She's talking to you.

Bubble Oh! Oh, all right.

Saffron I'll make up the spare room for you.

Bubble Thanks.

scene five Aeroplane

Flight to St Tropez. Edina and Patsy are sitting next to each other.

Edina God, I needed this break.

Patsy is being served drinks off trolley. An Air France air hostess moves on.

Patsy Oi! Peanuts. Sullen, stingy, bloody French bitch.

Air hostess returns with complimentary nuts.

Air Hostess Madame ...

Patsy ... moiselle. Merci. Et un autre whisky ... Et un autre gin.

Edina Not for me, Patsy.

Patsy No, for me, darling. Do you want anything?

Edina Orange juice. I'm going to have a healthy week. I'm not drinking and I'm not eating.

Patsy Right.

Edina Well, just fruit. I'm not drinking and I'm eating just fruit.

Patsy Well, you can't go to France and not drink. The chateau is in the middle of a vineyard. The air alone is fifteen per cent proof.

Edina Well, just wine. No spirits. Drink just wine, eat just fruit and not smoke. Good.

Patsy And I'm not having sex.

Edina Right. Sure?

Patsy Positive.

Edina Good. Done. Santé.

Patsy Santé.

Edina When do we start? Now or when we land?

Patsy Well . . . *(Looks up and down the aisle.)* I think I could safely start now. *(Man comes out of toilet. Walks past her seat.)* But let's say, when we land.

Edina Good. Give me a ciggy.

`scene six` Edina's Kitchen

Mother *(Comes downstairs.)* Having trouble finding BBC, dear. I flicked through fifteen channels. *(Gives Saffron the remote control.)*

Saffron It's on satellite. Press this one. *(Shows her the button.)*

Mother Right O. I kept seeing Italian housewives taking off their bras and I thought this can't be *Challenge Anneka*. You don't mind if I have a sherry, do you, dear? *(Goes to fridge.)* Or shall I have a Japanese beer? *(Takes one out. Examines it.)* No.

`scene seven` France

Long straight rural road at dusk. Small hire car speeds past, brake lights on. It swerves to a halt on the wrong side of the road. Edina gets out of the driving seat.

Edina Am I on the wrong side or the right side of the road? Wake up, Patsy, I can't go on till I'm sure.

Patsy *(Emerges.)* Keep driving, Eddy. You haven't hit anything, yet.

Edina There hasn't been anything to hit for the past hour, Patsy. We're so lost, there isn't even any other traffic!

Patsy I know exactly where we are.

Edina Right. Here's the steering wheel, so imagine we're on the road. We're going to overtake, I'd go this way, therefore – no! Hang on! Is this left-hand drive? God, it's so long since I drove a car. Which hand do I change gear with in England? No, no, no . . . I should be driving on the right-hand side.

Patsy Are you all right? Would you like me to take over?

Edina So speaks the woman whose head has been lolling around like a bladder on a stick for the best part of the journey.

They get into the car.

Edina Just stay awake and look at the map. Read the instructions.

Patsy Leave airport, turn right . . . Bla, bla, bla.

Car sets off.

Edina No . . . right. Right is the same in France, isn't it. I shouldn't have gone left, should I?

scene eight French Farmhouse

It is very late at night. The farmhouse is very run down, but with pretty possibilities, charming but rough. There are insects, mice, etc. It is very dusty, stocked as a holiday home – odd puzzles, games, packs of cards, lots of books, old furniture, original sink and kitchen, old gas cooker. There is the sound of a car pulling up outside. Headlights switch off. Farmhouse door opens, and Patsy and Ed stagger in through pouring rain with luggage. Patsy is scraping a squashed snail off her shoe. They switch on the light, and stand aghast. It is not quite what they had in mind. Patsy tries her best.

Patsy It's gorgeous.

Edina After eight hours in that car with you, Pats, the local pissotière looked rather attractive. But this?! Shut up.

Patsy Oh, shut up and sit down.

Edina Eight hours, Patsy. Well, that kind of knocks your idea of wild nightlife in St Tropez on the head.

Patsy It only took that long because you, Eddy, insisted on retracing the whole bloody route back to the airport every time I gave you a bloody instruction.

Edina We wouldn't have had to if you hadn't insisted that every village we'd been through was called Clochmerle.

Patsy We've been round in so many bloody circles, thanks to you, we might only be ten minutes from St Tropez.

Edina (*Sulkily.*) I don't think so, Patsy. The sky lost that comforting orange glow a long way back, babe. (*She is wandering around inspecting the kitchen. She picks up a pan, screams and drops it.*) Cockroaches! Oh, my god, and a mouse. Oh, my god. Oh, my god!

Patsy Don't worry, darling. Where did they go?
She grabs a broom. There is a great deal of banging and flapping.

Edina Don't kill them. I'm a Buddhist. I could come back as one of those.

Patsy Out they go. I think the cockroach had a coronary, darling.

Edina (*Slamming door shut.*) Oh, god . . .

Patsy Let's have a drink and fix something to eat.

Edina There are four pieces of old pasta and half a packet of French toast that defies eating at the best of times.

Patsy (*Opens some drinks she's had from the plane.*) Here.

Edina I'm never going abroad again. Everywhere is riddled, infested with insects. They follow me everywhere from Tuscany to the Caribbean. Insects, insects, centipedes, snakes, mosquitoes, cockroaches. I look at pictures of luxurious mansions in Morocco and LA and I think 'Yes, but how big are your spiders?' You never see a picture of Jane Seymour with a centipede hanging off her tiara. They bite me, Pats. They never bite you.

Patsy The last one that bit me had to check in to the Betty Ford clinic.

Edina God, I hate France.

Patsy *(Trying to make the best of it.)* Look, Eds, we're in Provence. Everybody is coming to Provence. Tomorrow we'll stroll into the local village and buy croissant, fresh ground coffee, and local vino, a light white wine. We'll crack open whole baguettes and stuff them with camembert and brie. We'll wander to local markets and sniff melons. We'll sit outside in big straw hats, long shirts, slacks, and espadrilles. We'll look like Ava Gardner, and . . . *(She can't think of an Edina equivalent.)* . . . her companion.

There is a roll of thunder and the lights go out.

Edina Straw dogs!

Patsy Don't panic. I've got a lighter.

Edina *(Ranting.)* Why does this always happen? Only abroad! The suggestion of a thunderstorm and all the lights go out. Let's all join Europe so that the lights can all go out – Sieg Heil . . . the Federal State!

Patsy Shut up, Eddy. *(Lights a lighter. Lights a candle.)* What is the matter with you? You need a joint. We both need a joint.

Edina I haven't got any. Saffy flushed it. Everything. Haven't you got some?

Patsy I was counting on you. I've got a bit of coke and some ecstasy.

Edina No one's taking ecstasy any more. *(Swigs the brandy.)* Let's go to bed.

scene nine Small Bedroom

A rickety double bed. Patsy and Edina enter.

Patsy There's only one candle. I'll sleep here, too.

Edina Check under the bed ... In the bed ... Behind the bed. Pull it away from the wall and don't let the covers touch the floor ...

They get into bed fully dressed, and blow out the candle. Everything is dark and silent.

Edina *(Quietly.)* Something the size of a hand just crawled across my face.

Silence.

66

67

Patsy That was my hand. Sorry, Eddy.

scene ten Farmhouse Kitchen

It is morning. A beautiful day makes the whole place look better. Sun is streaming through the windows. Patsy is standing looking out of the door. Edina enters spraying huge can of fly spray, clutching a dustpan and brush.

Edina I'm sorry about the ozone layer, but this is a matter of survival. Pats, you go down the village. You know what we need.

Patsy I don't know what we need.

Edina Darling! Bread, croissant, cafe, oeufs, milk, lots of lovely French things. I'll write it down for you. We need ...

(Writes.) Bread . . .

Patsy From the, er . . . ?

Edina Bakery, the Painerie.

Patsy Blancemangerie?

Edina No, franagerie. No, Potage. No, that's soup. Oh, you'll see it. It'll be in the window. Boucherier is butcher, isn't it?

Patsy Mangerie?

Edina No, look, ask. Ou est c'est possible de comprends des pains? Right! What's milk?

Patsy Let – late.

Edina Where do we get that from?

Patsy Delicatessen?

Edina Vegetables a la grocerie. Right?

Patsy You go.

Edina Oh all right. Will you ring and let Saffy and Bubble know we're here.

Patsy I've tried. I can't work out the bloody code.

Edina What is it from LA? It must be the same.

Patsy It doesn't work, and there isn't a book.

Edina Ring the operator.

Patsy And say what?

Edina What's the code for England, Londra.

Patsy I'll try when you've gone.

Edina I'm off.

Patsy Got money?

Edina Yes, I've got a few five-hundred franc notes.

Patsy Is that enough?

Edina Five-hundred pounds, Pats. *(Thinks.)* I've got cards, too.
I should be all right.

*Edina ties on a huge straw hat over her Vivienne Westwood smock
and leggings, and sets off. No sooner has she gone than there is a
knock on the door. Patsy answers. It is a very small toothless Frenchman
in old suit. He gabbles something in French. It is impossible to
understand. Patsy is confused and tries to shoo him away. She ends up
getting him some money and shutting the door on him. She then goes
to the phone and rings the operator. We hear the operator answer,
speaking very fast. Patsy panics, blows a huge raspberry and puts
phone down. She then proceeds to dial different combinations of numbers
in the hope of finding the code for London.*

scene eleven Small French village

68
69

*The village is very quiet, no apparent sign of life. Everything must be
happening indoors. A couple of old women, dressed in black, are sitting
on a crate outside a house. There is a dog asleep in road and a bicycle
with panniers full of baguettes leaning against a wall. There are no
obvious shops, but lots of doors with heavy plastic stripping which might
or might not be a shop. Edina pulls up in car and gets out. She is
immediately out of place. She wanders up and down trying to be
confident. She thinks about asking the old women for help, but decides
against it. She parts the plastic strips on one doorway, sniffs, but sees
nothing. It is dark inside, and there is the noise of flies buzzing. She
doesn't go in. She looks in at another doorway. It is a bar – very dark
inside. A couple of old men and a small child stare at her from within.
The barman is watching TV. She doesn't go in. She considers stealing
the baguettes from the bicycle, but doesn't. She gives up.*

scene twelve Farmhouse

Patsy is still dialling. Edina is eating French toast.

Patsy I must be getting closer.

Edina I'll get Saffy to come over and buy the food.

Patsy Get her just to send the food. She could ring up the shop in French and get them to deliver.

There is a knock at door. Edina opens it.

Edina Patsy, come here quickly.

Patsy goes to door. Standing in the doorway is the old man with no teeth.

Patsy Oh, no.

The old man starts talking, but Edina and Patsy cannot understand what he is saying.

Edina What does he want?

Patsy Push off!! *(She shrugs in a French sort of way, and closes the door.)* I've forgotten where I got up to.

Edina Four-Nought . . .

Patsy resumes dialling.

scene thirteen Edina's Kitchen

Mother is reading Take a Break, *Saffy is reading* New Statesman.

Mother Ah, here's another you'll know.

Saffron Not another competition.

Mother It's all competitions . . . I've never won a big prize, but I've got eight keyrings and a foot-spa at home that say I'm on the right track. Now. Multiple choice. Oh! Now. *(Grabs Saffron's arm. Saffron is desperately bored, trying to read.)* Now. Multiple choice. *(Looks for instructions.)* Here we are. Multiple choice. 'Find the answer, that you think or know is correct out of the choices given and enter that letter' . . . Meaning, I suppose, though it doesn't say so, the letter . . .

Saffron I understand. I understand. Just ask the question.

Mother *(Making a lot of fuss with spectacles and pen, etc.)* Right. Okay. Here we go. To win a holiday in the Cayman Islands. A fantasy . . .

Saffron What's the question?

Mother Right. How long was Margaret Thatcher Prime Minister for? a) 11 Years; b) 500 Years; c) 2 Months; d) 2000 Years. Well, I think we can rule out the last one quite happily.

The intercom buzzes, and Saffron picks up phone.

Mother So, A, B or C?

Bubble It's me.

Bubble enters rushing across the hall into the kitchen in a panic.

Bubble Has she rung?

Saffron No. What's the matter?

Bubble It's very urgent. Very angry man needs her to sign summat, or doings's flat won't be seen to.

Saffron Can't it wait?

Bubble It's cutting it really, really, fine, if I wait till she gets back. I think he wants it on his desk tomorrow pronto. This sort of thing has never happened to me before.

Saffron You've never done anything before.

Bubble I know. I don't know why she wants to do this interior design thing . . . There's just so much work.

Mother And she never will be told. Always had her own ideas about decorating. How she could live in her room at home still amazes me. I mean it's had two coats of paint and three different wallpapers on since she left home, but if the light's right I can still see Jimi Hendrix's face staring out at me. *(Mother starts to* *sing.)* Purple haze all in my brain, familiar faces just ain't the same. *(Pauses.)* Oh, it's B.

The phone rings. Saffron answers.

Saffron Mum! Why? . . . How can you have malnutrition?

scene fourteen Farmhouse Kitchen

The doorbell rings. Patsy opens the door, and Saffron is there with huge box of provisions. Bubble is lurking in the background.

Patsy Wine. Thank god. *(Pulls bottle of wine from box.)* Eddy, Eddy. Rosemary's Baby has arrived with food.

They enter. Edina rushes in.

Edina Food! Hurrah! Wine! *(Grabs the box.)* Sweetie. *(As an afterthought.)* Hallo.

Edina hasn't noticed Bubble who is looking nervous. Patsy has opened the wine and is swigging from the bottle before pouring into glasses.

Saffron This isn't really what I imagined.

Edina Awful, isn't it?

Saffron I like it.

Edina It's been a nightmare. Have you eaten?

Saffron No.

Edina Right. I'll throw something together for lunch.

Saffron A sandwich would do.

Edina No, darling. I'll do one of my specials. Throw some garlic and tomatoes into some olive oil and toss in a few herbs. Pass me a pan.

Bubble passes a pan. Edina freezes. She hasn't noticed her before.

Bubble Bonjour.

scene fifteen Farmhouse Kitchen

Everybody but Saffron, is eating a horrible tomato mush on bread. Saffron is making a sandwich.

Edina Bruschetta! It's Bruschetta!

Saffron Bubble, do you want a sandwich?

Edina Oh, suddenly very pally.

Saffron Mum, she speaks excellent French and I needed some company.

Bubble *(To Eddy.)* I thought you spoke French?

Edina I do. But not this impossible local dialect. I speak Parisian French.

Saffron That's just English spoken rather loudly with a sour look on your face.

Edina Don't be ridiculous. Mia' accento e perfetto.

Patsy *(Eyes closed.)* Smell that air!

scene sixteen Farmhouse Garden

Saffron is reading a book, Bubble is playing a confused game of patience, Edina and Patsy are at a loose end.

Edina Got a ciggy? *(Patsy throws her a packet of Gitannes.)* This takes me back, Pats. Soft packet of French cigarettes. Do you remember the routine? *(She rips off the corner of the packet, taps the packet to loosen the cigarettes, and flicks it so they come out of the hole. She takes one, rolls it in her fingers, taps one end on the table, smells it, then puts it in her mouth. The paper sticks horrifically to her lip.)* Pats, help. It's stuck.

Patsy leans over and pulls it off.

Edina Ow! Ow! You've taken half my lip with it.

Saffron Anyone want a game of table tennis?

Silence.

Edina I'm sorry there's nothing to do, darling.

Saffron What do you mean? There's plenty to do. You could read, or play a game, or paint, or have a game of table tennis.

Edina Darling, that's all right if you're a deprived child at its first youth club.

Patsy Or a Prisoner from Cell Block H.

Edina But I was hoping for a heated pool.

Saffron *(To Bubble.)* Table tennis?

Bubble Oh, yeah. Hope I can remember how to play.

They exit.

Patsy *(To Edina.)* Do you want to drop a tab of ecstasy. *(Holds up tab.)*

Edina Not with Saffy here. And anyway, darling, I hear it's dangerous. People are carried out of raves bleeding from every orifice.

Patsy We wouldn't go to a rave . . . just a cafe.

Edina No, Pats. I know it's just a chemical and wouldn't be hurting any South Americans, but no!

Patsy Coke?

Edina No, Pats.

Patsy Do you mind if I do?

Edina Do whatever you want.

Patsy She doesn't frighten me.

Saffron enters. Patsy throws the ecstasy as far away as she can.

scene seventeen Farmhouse Garden

Edina is at easel painting idyllic rural scene. Patsy is drinking Champagne and reading Paris Match, *Bubble is doing jigsaw puzzle. Saffron is walking past Edina.*

Edina Darling, if you want to borrow some *old* jeans there's some in my case.

Saffron These are my old jeans.

Edina No, darling. You know *old* jeans! In my case.

Saffron You mean Stonewashed.

Edina Don't be stupid, sweetie, you wouldn't be allowed into France with Stonewashed jeans. I mean, old jeans.

Saffron These are my . . .

Edina Saffy. There are some old Levi 501s on my bed. I wish you would put them on.

scene eighteen Farmhouse

All four are playing Monopoly.

Bubble I'm broke.

Patsy Well, take out another mortgage. Don't give in.

Bubble On Kings Cross Station?

Saffron *(To Patsy.)* I thought you were broke? Where did you get all that money from?

Patsy *(Huge stash beside her.)* Don't question me.

Saffron Where did you get it?

Patsy I borrowed it from the bank.

Saffron You can't do that. That's cheating.

Patsy Listen, snake-eyes. I own Park Lane. I can borrow as much money as I like.

Edina *(To Saffron.)* Try and get into the spirit of the thing, Saff.

scene nineteen Farmhouse Terrace

It is early evening. Saffron and Edina are on the terrace.

Saffron It's lovely here.

Edina Lovely, yes.

Saffron How can you not be enjoying it? It's so peaceful, relaxing . . . just walking and reading and playing games. It's fun.

Edina Fun. I can see it should be, sweetie, and I know it should be, but I just can't feel it. It's like a secret that I know exists, but I'm not in on. Your sort of fun.

scene twenty Wine Cave

Edina and Patsy are tasting wine, bottle after bottle. They are getting drunker and drunker. Whole bottles are consumed. They eventually slide, disgracefully drunk, under the table with wine dribbling from their mouths.

scene twenty-one Farmhouse

Edina is sitting at table with jigsaw puzzle. Patsy appears, rubbing her nose. There is the sound of table tennis being played in the background.

Edina *(Indicating puzzle.)* You do the grass. I'll do the sky.

Patsy Okay.

Bubble appears holding bats.

Bubble Do you want to play doubles.

Edina Oh, no. I can't play.

Patsy Only if I can play with Eddy.

scene twenty-two Farmhouse Table Tennis Room

Edina and Patsy very reluctantly agree to play doubles. In a series of time-lapsed shots, they gradually become more and more competitive as their true spirits emerge. Saffron and Bubble eventually give up. It has become table tennis to the death.

scene twenty-three Farmhouse

There is the noise of furious table tennis being played. Saffron and Bubble are packing up cases and moving them to the door. Saffron comes across a piece of paper and reads it.

Saffron Isn't this the paper you wanted my mother to sign?

Bubble *(Freezing.)* Oh, jeepers-creepers!

Saffron Go and give it to her now. There's still time.

Bubble No. *(Pauses.)* You.

Saffron Go on. *(She pushes Bubble to door. Edina screams, then appears panicked and furious. Patsy and Bubble follow.)*

Edina Get me to that telephone. *(Goes to phone.)*

Saffron *(To Bubble.)* I'd wait in the car if I were you.

Patsy and Bubble exit.

scene twenty-four Outside Farmhouse

As Patsy and Bubble are putting cases in the car they are approached by the toothless old man. He speaks to Patsy.

Bubble *(Translating.)* He says he's wondering why we have been staying in the cottage. The staff have been expecting us at the Chateau half a mile down the road. He hopes we had a pleasant stay.

Patsy is shocked into a moment's silence.

Patsy *(To Bubble.)* Listen, you goat, if you repeat this to anybody, I'll kill you.

Edina rushes screaming from the house.

Edina Drive! Just drive!

scene twenty-five **Airport**
Customs Hall
Bubble and Saffron are waiting as Edina and Patsy are searched.

Patsy Absolutely ridiculous. Stopping me! Look at the people you're letting through stoned. Chinese hippies with backpacks, for god's sake.

Edina There is someone waiting just by the barrier to take this piece of paper and save my reputation and career.

There is no response. The customs officer searches Patsy's bag. She is getting nervous. Edina is looking at her, anxiously.

Edina *(Whispering.)* Now, Pats. If they find anything, you're on your own.

The customs officer finds something.

Customs officer Can I ask you whose bag this is?

Patsy It's my bag.

Customs officer *(Reading tag.)* Edina Monsoon.

Edina My bag? That's not my sponge bag.

Patsy I'm saying nothing, until I see my lawyer.

Customs officer Who packed this bag?

Edina and Patsy both turn together and point at Saffron and Bubble.

Edina and Patsy They did.

scene twenty-six Small Interview Room at Customs

All four are sitting in stony silence. Saffron is staring hard at Edina.

Edina You don't need to say anything.

Saffron I know.

Edina *(To Bubble.)* If you'd given me that piece of paper earlier I would have rushed home sooner and I wouldn't be sitting here now.

Saffron It's not her fault that we are sitting here.

Edina Can you comprehend the scale of what's happening here? Do you know what it means? It means Bettina's flat won't be finished and this is the end of my new-found career in interior design.

Saffron Buildings everywhere might heave a sigh of relief.

Edina *(To Bubble.)* I don't know why I don't just sack you.

Bubble starts to cry.

Saffron Don't be silly. Where else are you going to find someone that makes doing nothing into an art form? *(To Bubble.)* Sorry I had to say that.

Bubble It's all right. I didn't quite understand what you meant.

Patsy has turned very pale and is shaking.

Patsy Is no one going to say anything to me? Don't talk to me, anybody. I'm the one that's going to go to prison.

Bubble At least, you got your table tennis practice in.

Man and woman customs officers appear.

Patsy I need to call my lawyer. I must be allowed to make that call before my freedom is taken from me.

78 | 79

Male officer That won't be necessary Miss Stone. The white powder we found was a perfectly harmless, innocent substance. You are all free to go.

Patsy I beg your pardon.

Male officer You are free to go.

Patsy Just hang on there. I demand you retest it.

The man and woman officer leave.

Patsy Come back here. I paid a huge amount of money for that. Don't you tell me it's talcum powder.

Edina Come on, darling. So you were diddled. It's happened to us all once in a while. But let's get moving.

Patsy Oh, god . . . It's not the money, Eddy.

Edina What is it?

Patsy It's the horrible realization that I must have actually enjoyed playing ping-pong!

Cast List

Edina · JENNIFER SAUNDERS

Patsy · JOANNA LUMLEY

Saffron · JULIA SAWALHA

Bubble · JANE HORROCKS

Mother · JUNE WHITFIELD

Tony (Headmaster) · TIM WOODWARD

Sarah · NAOKO MORI

Joanna · LISA COLEMAN

James · ADRIAN ROSS-MAGENTY

Daniel · JAMES LANCE

School Secretary · TRICIA AILEEN

Teacher No. 1 · PAUL MARK ELLIOTT

Teacher No. 2 · SIDNEY COLE

Headmistress · ANNABEL HAMPSON

scene one Isolation Tank in Edina's Bathroom

Edina is looking at the gently-lit roof of her isolation tank, which is flickering with the reflection of the water. There is the sound of breathing. A mobile telephone comes into view. Edina presses digits.

scene two Edina's Kitchen

Saffron is sitting at kitchen table with a group of her friends. Sarah is a grim girl, Joanna is a grimmish girl and James is a very straight boy (a Saffy equivalent). They are involved in some science project together. Phone rings. Saffron answers.

scene three Inside the Isolation Tank

Edina *(On phone.)* Saffy, are you still in the house ... good. I'm in the isolation tank in my bathroom. Don't leave the house without telling me. I'm going to see if I can last another fifteen minutes.

scene four Edina's Kitchen

Saffron on the phone to Edina. The others are talking, making tea, etc.

Saffron A call came through for Patsy, but I couldn't find her.

scene five Inside the Isolation Tank

Still seen from Edina's point of view.

Edina Patsy, there's a call come through for you.

(The camera tilts over, and we see Patsy, fag in mouth, lying next to Edina.)

Patsy Right. *(Puts fag out in tank.)* I'd better go, Eddy. You're going to have to be able to do it on your own sooner or later.

Patsy opens the lid of the tank and gets out.

Edina Don't close the lid, Pats. Don't close the door. Leave it open. Talk to me.

scene six Edina's Bathroom
Edina and Patsy, in bath robes, are drying off and looking at the tank.

Edina It's great, isn't it. You can't get them over here. It cost me a fortune to get it shipped from LA. Nobody else has got one.

scene seven Edina's Kitchen
Saffron, Joanna, Sarah and James are drinking tea and reading and writing and fiddling with molecule models. Saffron is pressing door answerphone button.

Saffron I don't think it would be wise to relate it all to the DNA structure too early.

The others nod seriously.

James It's important, too, with a demonstration of this nature to keep it simple and straightforward for those listening.

Joanna Even though we know it's really rather complicated and difficult.

Sarah Yes. *(Blushes slightly.)*

Daniel enters. He is rich and scruffy. James groans slightly, the girls perk up, Sarah blushes a bit more.

Daniel Hi, look, sorry I'm so late.

Saffron That's okay. We were just about to take a break and have some lunch.

Daniel Massive house!

Saffron Well, it's not really big . . . It's actually just on a lot of

82
83

floors. I mean, it is semi-detached. They're all the same in this area.

Daniel Well. Great area.

Saffron Well, yes, my mother bought it before it was nice though. Then everybody else started living here. I mean Sarah lives just up the road.

Sarah *(Blushes a bit and looks down.)* Yes. *(She looks madly in bag for something to cover her embarrassment.)*

Daniel Where we live, really, it's actually just workman's cottages and council flats.

Joanna Where's that?

Daniel Chelsea.

James groans.

Daniel I mean, there's quite a few homeless people living down our street. You know so . . .

Joanna So . . . what?

Daniel So . . . I think when I finish college I'm going to work with homeless people.

James I thought you were going to be an investment banker.

Daniel That's just what pop wants me to do.

Edina and Patsy enter.

Saffron Oh, no! *(Gives Edina a black look.)*

Edina Watch out, Pats, we are now entering a 'no fun' zone.

Patsy A coven.

Edina *(To Saffy.)* Don't look so worried, darling. We're just coming down to grab a bite of lunch, then we'll take it upstairs. We'll just grab some dry bread and a cup of water and scuttle back upstairs.

Daniel *(To Edina and Patsy.)* Hi. I'm Daniel.

Edina and Patsy are taken aback by the sight of a good-looking male in Saffron's presence.

Edina *(Flirting hideously.)* Well, hallo. *(Looking approvingly at Saffron.)*

Patsy *(Flirting even more hideously.)* Danny, hallo.

Edina Don't let us disturb you all. *(Nudges Saffy and goes to the fridge.)* Can I offer anybody a drink? Boys? Anything you fancy? Danny?

Daniel Well, yeah, I'll have a Bud.

Edina *(To James.)* You?

James Well, I'll have a . . . er . . . *(He can't think of anything.)* Er . . . Bud . . . yes. Thank you.

Edina throws them both a beer.

Edina The sisters Grimm, can I tempt you?

Saffron We don't drink, Mum.

Edina Pats? *(Pulls out bottle of Champagne.)* Okay?

Patsy nods.

Saffron *(Coming up close to Edina.)* What are you doing here? You should be in the office now. You're hanging around as if you are on holiday.

Edina I know, sweetie. I've got more time on my hands than I know what to do with. Bubble's doing everything.

Saffron Bubble!

Edina I sent Bubble to an occupational hypnotist and since she came back she's . . . well . . . she's like a PA. Copes with everything. Extraordinary. *(Pauses.)* Pats, do you want to finish off this beluga or just have some smoked salmon on something?

84
85

Patsy Whatever.

Saffron is very embarrassed.

Edina Are you lot all right with just bread and cheese? Have anything you want. Whole house at your disposal.

Saffron We're all right.

Edina *(Moving over to other side of kitchen.)* Pats and I will just stand here and you won't know we're here.

Saffron and her friends sit round table eating and working.

Saffron Sorry about that.

James It's okay. We understand.

Joanna and Sarah nod grimly. Daniel is looking at Patsy, who is winking at him.

Joanna Can we go over again how many molecule structures we are going to use and . . .

Champagne cork pops.

Edina Sssssh, Pats.

Joanna . . . How many we are going to reconstruct? *(She is interrupted again by Edina talking to Patsy.)*

Edina You know Jane's divorce has gone through.

Patsy Thank bloody god.

Edina Now they're just fighting over the *Hello!* magazine contract.

Patsy What's the money? How much are they offering?

Edina Well, that's the thing. They're only offering thirty-five grand and she's willing to throw in the children.

Patsy Must be worth more . . . ? Her at home and the children?

Edina And he's only got a dog and a house in LA, and a pool.

Patsy They like a pool. It ups the glam quotient.

Saffron Mum! Keep it down, please.

Edina Sorry, darling.

Patsy *(In loud whispers.)* Do you want to know some gossip about someone you don't know?

Edina Of course. *(Looks at watch.)* Tell me on the way to the office. We're off, sweetie. *(Crosses over to kiss Saffron.)* Bye, bye, sweetie.

Saffron *(Noticing the fish eggs round Edina's mouth.)* It's like kissing a spawning sturgeon.

Edina No, sweetie, I like having eggs in my mouth.

Patsy It's the only place she's got them.

Edina Me and my ovaries are leaving.

Patsy and Edina exit.

Saffron Sorry.

Daniel She's great.

The others look disapprovingly at him.

scene eight Edina's Offices

Patsy and Edina enter outer office.

Patsy . . . I don't know what happened after that. I had to hang up. She was crying too much. But I'll ring back and get the rest of the story.

Edina Tell her what I said. I'm sure she wouldn't mind that I know.

They enter main office.

Edina Right, I'm here. Don't panic. What's to be done?

Bubble is sitting at Edina's desk.

Bubble I'll just finish signing these, then get out of your way.

Edina Do you need me to sign some?

Bubble No, that's it now. *(Gets up.)* Have you had lunch?

Edina Oh, er, yes. Listen. We've had lunch.

Bubble I'll get some coffee and wine or Champagne sent in.

Edina Yes, yes. Look, we'll need some of that.

Bubble exits. Edina is at a loose end, trying to find something to do or make a fuss about. The phone rings.

Edina Oh, god! *(Lights a fag.)* Here we go!

Bubble Got it.

Phone rings off. Bubble has taken the call in outer office. Edina flaps through paper on desk, rearranges piles. Secretary enters with Champagne and magazines.

Bubble *(From outer office.)* You might like to look through this month's selection while I prepare your diary.

Edina Yes, good.

Edina and Patsy sip Champagne and flick through magazines. Edina is restless, Patsy unperturbed.

Edina Look, I haven't got time to flick through magazines. I can't live my life as if I'm at the hairdresser's.

Patsy Do you want me to ring Diane and get the rest of the story? She must have stopped blubbing by now.

Edina Later.

Patsy Shall we have a bitch through *Hello!* magazine and the *Enquirer*?

Edina No, Pats.

Patsy But, darling, Priscilla Presley. Katherine Oxenberg. *(No reaction.)* Liz Taylor . . . *(No reaction.)* . . . Khashoggi . . . Shahpari Khashoggi . . . All that money and she's still got a moustache. It's lucky there's a staple there, or she'd be all over the carpet. Look, darling, one more face lift and she'd have a beard. Look at this tack. It's so expensive it looks cheap. And, darling, why do we think Priscilla Presley wears gloves?

Edina I don't know, Pats.

Patsy Liver spots . . . Don't you remember?

Edina Where's Bubble? Bubble. *(Bubble enters.)* Look, what's happening?

Bubble I'll just go through a few of the things in the diary for this week. Charity, Emporio, Armani, drinks, lunch, launch, Gucci opening. Invites for fashion show, Westwood, Hamnett, Betty Jackson, Richmond shows. Said 'yes' to all. You do Westwood. Party, party. Koo Stark is having a retrospective of work she has yet to do; drinks, press call. Book launches – Bill Wyman, *Coping With Cystitis*. Press call. Ribs at 'Sticky Fingers'. Party, party, party. Paula Yates *If I can't have a career why should they?* Party. She will be expressing milk throughout. Linda McCartney, Emma Freud, Joan Collins, Marie Helvin. Ivana Trump, launch of her new perfume 'the smell that lingers longer than he does'. Tokyo, Hong Kong, New York, Paris, Milan.

Edina Did Bruce call?

Bubble Yes, just for a chat . . . so I had a chat. Didn't want to bother you. The rest is all very bottom of the league. Esther Rantzen, Simon Bates, Chris Tarrant, Amanda de Cadenet.

Secretary enters.

Secretary Your car's here.

Bubble Right. Got to dash. Got everything you need? I'm on the mobile. *(Exits.)*

Edina *(In shock.)* I am surplus to my own life.

scene nine Edina's Kitchen

It is early evening. The Saffy gang are still at it. James, Joanna and Sarah are starting to pack up. Edina and Patsy enter.

Edina *(Still moping.)* Hallo, Saffron, sweetie.

Saffron Hi. *(She continues talking to her friends.)* Okay, if you come round tomorrow we'll have one more day before the presentation.

Edina The ... what ... darling?

Saffron It doesn't matter, Mum.

Patsy *(To Edina.)* Don't let her talk to you like that, Eddy. Tell her she's adopted.

Saffron What?

Edina Nothing, dear. It doesn't matter.

All the friends leave except Daniel.

Patsy Can I just do one thing that's really been annoying me. *(She goes up to molecule and adjusts it. Daniel and Saffron are impressed.)*

Edina There's nothing you can tell Patsy about arranging balls. She was always very good at genetics.

Saffron I'm not surprised. She's been a walking sperm bank most of her life.

Daniel Well, I must be off.

Edina *(To Saffron.)* Would you like us to leave the room?

Saffron We are just friends.

Daniel Bye. *(Exits.)*

Edina *(Without looking up.)* Bye, Pats.

Patsy Goodbye, Eddy. *(She exits after Daniel.)*

Edina *(To Saffron.)* Can I help you with your molecules, darling?

Saffron Please, don't touch them.

Edina Darling, we could be friends.

Saffron I've got friends.

Edina You can't mean those pieces of lichen that were here today. Honestly, when I think of the schools I sent you to . . . The interesting and creative people you could be with now if you'd stayed at them. Bedales, for god's sake. But no, you had to send yourself to the local grammar.

Saffron The people don't get more interesting the more money you lay out.

Edina They do. Couldn't you just rebel, for god's sake?

Saffron I thought I was.

Edina I mean, you and your generation . . . those little gremlins, the lichen people, what will you leave the world as your legacy? You'll never come up with anything original.

Saffron What did you ever leave? The lava lamp and the bean-bag?

Edina Darling, don't be so uptight.

Saffron I'm sorry if I don't want to loll around naked, painted dayglow, with a flower in every orifice, humping the air to Jefferson Airplane.

Edina It was the Grateful Dead. How is it at school, darling?

Saffron I'm not at school any more.

Edina Aren't you?

Saffron I'm at the sixth-form college.

Edina Is that a different place?

Saffron A different part of the building.

Edina Oh, a different part of the building. Oh! And this project you're doing?

Saffron Don't get involved.

Edina I'm your mother. I am interested.

Saffron No, you're not. You're bored.

Edina I want to know.

Saffron It's a DNA project that we present next week at the open day as part of our term work. All right?

Edina Open day? . . . Darling . . . ? Open day? . . . Sweetie . . . ? At your school. Sixth-form school – Poly – college thing . . . ? Is it . . . Saffy?

Saffron Don't. Please, Mum.

Edina Next week, sweetie? Which day?

Saffron You're not coming.

Edina I am, sweetie.

Saffron Mum, please don't.

Edina You have to let me, darling.

Saffron NO.

Edina Okay, okay . . . Forget about it. I see what you're saying . . . *(Pauses.)* I can't believe the way you treat me. After all I have done for you. I try so bloody hard to make your life wonderful. There isn't anything you couldn't have . . . There isn't anything I wouldn't let you do . . . Now you won't even let me come to your open day. Be nice, sweetie. I could get you all T-shirts made for your presentation. 'DLA Project' on them. Video screens, catering . . . Tell me what you need.

Saffron No.

Edina I'll get the sixth school college a swimming pool.

Saffron No. You are not coming and that is an end to it.

Edina I want to.

Saffron No.

Edina sulks, then throws wooden spoons onto the floor. When this has no effect, she bangs her head on kitchen counter, then lies on the floor kicking feet in two-year-old-type tantrum.

Edina I want to come. I want to come.

Gets up, realizing it hasn't had the desired effect.

Edina Sweetie, I'm going to my isolation tank now. I may be some time. *(Waits for effect.)* Bye, bye, darling. I could sink.

Saffron Not with your ballast.

Edina exits upstairs. We see her at top of stairs. There is no reaction from Saffron. She storms down again.

Edina I shall take some pills and kill myself.

Saffron Let me know how many . . .

Edina Yes, I will, darling.

Saffron . . . so I don't call the ambulance too soon.

Edina *(Thinks.)* If you don't let me come I'll adopt a Rumanian baby. That would be nice, wouldn't it.

Saffron Don't be so silly.

Edina *(Picks up mobile phone.)* I'm going to, sweetie. Now, I wonder who I'd call to do that. I'll ask Pats. You're forcing me to do this, darling. *(Looks at Saffron and dials.)*

Saffron No.

Edina What do they look like, Rumanians? Ah, Danny, is Pats there? What do Rumanians look like? *(She listens.)* Ivan Lendl. Oh? Thanks, darling.

Saffron You wouldn't dare. *(Realizing she is getting serious.)* It's a sick idea.

Edina A little baby, Saffy. That would give me something to do.

Saffron They wouldn't let you.

Edina I would be a bit like Mia Farrow. I could have more than one. I mean I always regretted not getting a Vietnamese one, when that was the thing. I could get one in every colour . . . one in every room.

Saffron It would last a day.

Edina That's rather a selfish thing to say, Saffy. Now, I wonder how one goes about it?

Saffron I should imagine you have to go to Rumania.

Edina Don't be silly. I'm sure they could send a selection over that I could choose from. I'll ring Bubble and get her on to it.

Saffron You wouldn't dare.

Edina I would.

Saffron Well, go on.

Edina presses digits without looking and speaks into phone.

Edina Bubble, if you've got a second, could you adopt me a Rumanian baby? Oh, you could. Get a selection and I'll pick some. Thank you, darling.

Edina and Saffron stare at each other.

Edina *(Going upstairs.)* La-la. La-la. La . . .

scene ten Edina's Hallway

Edina enters up kitchen stairs. She is obviously panicked, dialling madly.

Edina *(Into phone.)* Bubble? *(Pauses.)* What do you mean she's not taking any more calls? This is Edina. Edina Monsoon. I will not be put on hold . . . *(Dials again.)* Pats, emergency.

scene eleven Edina's Office

Edina and Patsy enter. Bubble is not to be seen.

Edina Where is she?

Patsy Where is the little tapeworm?

Secretary *(Entering.)* I'm sorry you can't just walk in like that. I might have to call security.

Patsy Piss off!

Edina You'll be calling yourself an ambulance in a minute. Come here. *(Grabs secretary.)* Where's Bubble?

Secretary She . . . she . . .

Patsy Let me smack her in the gob, Eddy!

Edina Where is she?

Secretary She's gone to New York.

Edina Did she leave a number . . . anything?

Secretary I don't know. She deals with everything.

Edina Did she leave a Rumanian number? Some clue?

The desk is empty.

Secretary Nothing. All I know is the Rumanian deal went through and the merchandise is on its way.

Patsy Get out.

Secretary exits.

Edina That can't be right. It can't happen this quickly, can it, Pats? I mean, shit! I don't want any babies. I didn't really ever want my own babies. I liked the idea of them all right, but the reality, Pats. The way they force you to think of someone else, nearly all the time.

Patsy Nightmare.

Edina You won't tell them I said that? I do love them now.

Patsy Course you do.

Edina I will be able to send them back.

Patsy You could sell them on . . . Mark them up and sell them on.

scene twelve Hallway

Patsy and Edina enter. Saffron is sitting on the stairs.

Patsy Calm down, Eddy. Come on, sweetie. *(Takes out box of pills.)* Throw a couple of these down you and it'll all seem much rosier. *(Sees Saffron on stairs and jumps.)* Oh, my god, there's something horrible on the stairs.

Saffron It's me.

Patsy I'm not blind.

Saffron What are those pills?

Patsy Don't question me.

Saffron Mum?

Edina They're hormones, darling, so I can breastfeed the Rumanians when they arrive.

Saffron Mum!

Patsy I'm off. See you tomorrow, Eddy.

Edina Meet you at Mothercare, Pats, ten o'clock.

Patsy Yes, darling.

Patsy exits.

Saffron You can stop it now.

Edina Stop what?

Saffron So you can stop pretending. I don't believe for a second that you would go through with this adoption just to get at me. But it did make me think. You can come to the presentation. And I don't mind. I'm sorry about the way I behaved before.

Edina Oh, right.

Saffron waits for Edina's reaction. There is none.

Saffron This is where we hug. Rumanian babies, huh!

Edina I know, darling. *(Gives Saffron a hug.)*

Saffron On two conditions. You never embarrass me beyond what is obviously unavoidable, and you don't get involved in the actual college.

Edina Of course not, darling. Thank you.

Edina walks up stairs looking worried. Saffy left at the bottom also looks worried.

Edina Rumanian babies! Silly old me. *(Pauses.)* Do you want a car or something?

Saffron No.

Edina continues upstairs, then turns again.

Edina Self-contained flat?

Saffron No.

Edina Night-night, darling. I do love you, despite what anyone might ever say, especially Patsy.

Saffron Goodnight.

scene thirteen Outside Saffron's College

Edina's car pulls up. Edina and Patsy and Mother get out. Edina is dressed as tastefully and as normally as she can bear. They stamp out their cigarettes and join a few parents on their way into the college. All the other parents are very ordinary grey people. Edina and Patsy smile patronizingly at them.

scene fourteen The School Corridor

Mother I'm really rather nervous.

Edina What on earth about?

Mother Something about the smell of schools. You've probably forgotten how many times I was summoned by your headmistress, for your smoking, or rudeness or truancy.

Edina Were we truant?

Mother Believe me, when I say that I think I spent more time at your school in that last year than either one of you.

Patsy Sexy smell, isn't it?

Edina Pats!

Patsy Takes me back. Testosterone mixed with cheap perfume. Biros, and folders and your first condom, which you'd hide in your desk with your Lucky Strike and Dr Whites.

Edina Great days.

Patsy Great days, Eddy.

Mother Here's Saffy.

Saffron greets them.

Edina Darling. We're here. Don't be nervous. Look. *(Shows her the tasteful outfit.)* Now, tell us where to go for the show.

Saffron It's not a show. It's a presentation.

Patsy Where's the bar?

Edina Pats, there isn't a bar. Is there, darling?

Saffron No.

Mother What's the talk about, dear?

Saffron DNA.

Mother Should that mean anything to me?

Saffron No.

Mother Good, as long as I know.

A teacher approaches.

Teacher 1 *(Looking at Mother.)* Saffron, is this your mother?

Saffron No, this is my mother. *(Indicating Edina.)*

Teacher 1 How do you do?

Edina Hallo.

Teacher 1 Look, the headmaster has asked me to round up some parents for him to meet, and send them along to his office.

Saffron shakes her head.

Teacher 1 There is a bit of time before the presentation. Would you like to come with me?

Saffron mouths 'No'.

Edina Well, can I bring my friend?

Teacher 1 Yes, of course.

They leave.

scene fifteen Corridor outside Headmaster's Office

Patsy and Edina are standing outside office. There is a light system for entry — red and green. The red light is on indicating that the headmaster is busy. The teacher comes out of office.

Teacher 1 I've told him you're here. He won't keep you.

The teacher leaves. Edina is getting nervous. She and Patsy become like two children summoned to the office.

Edina *(Whispering.)* Put that cigarette out, Pats.

Patsy *(Whispering.)* Why? I don't care. It's only a college.

Edina What do you think he wants to see us about?

Patsy I don't know, do I. It's you he wants to see.

Another teacher comes out of another office. He walks towards them, dressed as for 1967.

Teacher 2 Can I help you? What are you doing here?

Fade to flashback.

scene sixteen Flashback to 1967

Edina and Patsy are schoolgirls at school.

Patsy *(To second teacher.)* We're just waiting to see Miss Dines.

Teacher 2 Take that cigarette out of your mouth, Patricia Stone. You disgusting girl. You two make me sick. *(He leaves.)*

Patsy God, I hate him.

Edina Look, Pats, let's just stand here quietly. Please.

Patsy Here. *(Offers Edina a drag on her cigarette.)* Go on.

Edina I can't.

Patsy *(Forces Edina to take a drag, then puts it out.)* What do you think she'll say?

Edina *(Nearly in tears.)* I don't know, do I.

Patsy Don't you dare say anything about me and Tony.

Edina I won't.

Patsy *(Crawling.)* You know who you look like, Cathy McGowan.

Edina Do I?

Patsy Really pretty like her.

Edina *(More crawlingly.)* You look like Marianne Faithfull.

Patsy Do I?

A voice calls from the office.

Headmistress Come in now.

Patsy and Edina Oh, god . . . oh, god.

scene seventeen Headmistress' Office

Patsy and Edina enter. Tony, Patsy's boyfriend, is there. They stand in line in front of headmistress.

Headmistress You dirty, dirty, dirty, disgusting, revolting, devil children.

Patsy and Edina burst into tears.

Edina Not me. They were the ones having it off.

A buzzer sounds. Scene fades back to present day.

scene eighteen Corridor outside Headmaster's Office (Present Day)

Patsy and Edina slightly shocked by the sound of the buzzer.

Patsy and Edina Oh, god ... oh, god...

scene nineteen Headmaster's Office

Patsy and Edina enter. They meet the headmaster. It is Tony.

Tony *(Ignoring Edina.)* Patsy.

Patsy Tony.

Tony Er?

Edina Edina. Edina.

Tony *(To Patsy.)* Sherry?

scene twenty School Room

DNA presentation. Saffron, James, Joanna, Sarah and Daniel are ready to give their presentation. Mother is sitting with other parents ready. Edina enters, holds up T-shirt with DLA Project on it. Saffron declines it.

Edina Shall I sit here?

Saffron We're just waiting for Mr Simms to do the introduction.

Edina Oh.

Patsy and Tony enter. They have obviously been having a snog. They are a little bit tipsy. He has a lipstick-smeared face. Saffron is hideously embarrassed. Tony stands in front of group. Patsy stays leaning against door, glass and fag in hand, winking at Tony, and at Saffy.

Tony Right. Sorry to be delayed. Now ... *(turns to Saffron.)* What is it you're doing?

Saffron DNA.

Tony Well, take it away.

He leaves to join Patsy.

Saffron *(Fed up.)* Upper 6J have been doing a variety of science-based projects this year. Not all of them curriculum based.

Joanna DNA is composed of two intertwined strands, each consisting of a long linear sequence of nucleotides.

School Secretary *(Entering.)* Sorry, may I interrupt you? There is someone here to see Mrs Edina Monsoon.

Edina Oh, sorry. Sorry, Saffy. Don't wait for me.

She gets up leaving coat on chair. We see that the back of her very tasteful suit is gold lamé. She makes an exit. The presentation continues.

102

103

Sarah Genes are fundamental units of genetic information that correspond chemically ...

Edina enters holding a Rumanian baby.

Sarah ... to the sequence of nucleotides in a segment of DNA.

School secretary enters with another baby.

James A typical gene consists of hundreds of thousands of nucleotides only a few of which are shown here. The arrows show how the genetic formation in a portion of the nucleotide sequence—

A pram with four babies in it is pushed into the room.

Saffron *(Stops the presentation.)* Get out! Just get out!

Edina leaves, clutching babies. She passes Tony and Patsy now snogging. Teacher 1 approaches her.

Teacher 1 *(To Edina.)* We hope you'll be attending more open days and will become an active member of our PTA. Can I take you to see the foundations for our new General Studies rooms?

Edina *(Scene fades to Edina thrashing about having a nightmare.)* But I don't want to see the foundations . . .

Everything goes black.

scene twenty-one Edina's Bathroom

Edina *(From the darkness.)* No more open days . . . no more open days. Help, help. Oh, god. I'm dead. I'm blind.

The door of the isolation tank opens. Patsy's head appears.

Patsy Sorry, darling. I must just have knocked the door.

Edina *(Clambers out. She is in full wet suit.)* How long have I been in there? I was having a little rebirth then. How long have I been in there?

Patsy About thirty seconds, sweetie. You must have dozed off.

Edina *(Bemused, looks at tank.)* They're good, aren't they, Pats?

Patsy If you're the kind of girl that likes lying in a warm puddle.

Edina *(Thinks. Picks up the phone and dials.)* Bubble? It's me. Bubble what is your job?

Bubble *(On the phone.)* My job? I don't really know.

Fade to Edina in bathroom.

Edina What do you do?

Fade back to Bubble in the office.

Bubble *(On the phone.)* Nothing, really. Get paid.

Fade to Edina's bathroom.

Edina Good. (*Rings off.*)

Edina I had to import it from LA. No one else over here has got one.

Patsy I heard Fergie had one.

Edina Oh no, Oh no, Oh, I'll have to get rid of it now.

Patsy Are you going into the office?

Edina I . . .

scene twenty-two Edina's Kitchen

Saffron, Joanna, Sarah and James are working. Patsy and Edina enter.

Saffron Hi!

Edina Hallo, sweetie. Won't disturb you. Is Daniel here yet?

Saffron Daniel who?

Edina Thought that was a bit too good to be true.

Saffron Mum, you're not coming to the open day, are you?

Edina (*Laughs.*) I don't think so, darling. I don't think I'll have time.

They both turn away from each other with expressions of relief. Patsy and Edina have fish eggs and Champagne quickly.

Patsy Can we go to Yamishi's new shop on the way?

Edina Have you seen it?

Patsy Gorgeous window. Huge swathe of white chiffon and a terracotta pot.

Edina What does he sell?

Patsy White chiffon . . . terracotta pots. Maybe both.

Edina We'll go there quickly. I've got to fit in a high colonic and a body wax this afternoon. Let's go now and we can discuss Jane Fonda's tits on the way.

Patsy Do you want to hear a new joke? It's not in very good taste, but I heard that apparently Elizabeth Taylor is the new ride at Disneyland. *(They both laugh. Freeze.)*

birthday

Cast List

Edina · JENNIFER SAUNDERS

Patsy · JOANNA LUMLEY

Saffron · JULIA SAWALHA

Mother · JUNE WHITFIELD

Justin · CHRISTOPHER MALCOLM

Bo · MO GAFFNEY

Marshall · CHRISTOPHER RYAN

Oliver · GARY BEADLE

scene one **Edina's Bedroom**

It is morning. Edina is sitting up in bed. The blinds are closed, the room is dark. Julie Driscoll's 'Wheels on Fire' is playing faintly in the background. Edina is in a trance. Suddenly the blinds open, the room is light, the music stops. Saffron is at the window.

Saffron Morning. *(Comes up to the bed.)*

Edina Hallo death, hallo oblivion. What time is it?

Saffron Ten.

Edina I'd better be off.

Saffron It's Sunday.

Edina Oh! It's true, then.

Saffron *(Sits on bed. She has a package in her hand and some letters.)* Happ . . .

Edina Please don't.

Saffron Happy Birthday!

Edina How old am I? No, don't say it. I'm . . . I'm . . .

Saffron You're forty.

Edina breaks down dramatically.

Edina But . . . *(Weeping.)* . . . I don't feel forty.

Saffron You don't look . . . *(She hesitates, realizing she does.)*

Edina Thank you.

Saffron Come on, now. It's not the end of the world. It's just a day like any other day.

Edina It's as if I hit an oil patch at thirty-five and now I'm skidding towards the grave. Do I look different? Look at my face, sweetie. What do you see? Who do you see? *(Pauses.)* You may lie, darling. I'm just looking for a response.

Saffron Look, get Patsy to do this – she's better at it. I don't even know what a good lie would be. You look like a forty-year-old-woman who's just woken up.

Edina But I haven't been to sleep! I could feel the fortiness coming upon me in the night. I couldn't sleep. Go and look out of the blind, sweetie. I don't know if it's just my imagination, but I swear I can hear buzzards circling.

Saffron Do you want my present and these cards, now, or later?

Edina I don't know.

Saffron They might cheer you up.

Edina They might. What did you say?

Saffron Look, never mind.

Edina No, tell me, sweetie. You see, I didn't catch what you said. It takes longer for the messages to reach the brain of older people. Old ears, sweetie.

Saffron Right! *(Stands up.)* Now, listen to me. Old ears or not, try and concentrate. It is your birthday and you have the choice whether to make this hell for yourself and everybody else, to sulk and feel sorry for yourself, or get up, cheer up and enjoy the day.

Edina It feels like the end of my life. If my mother hadn't uncrossed her legs so early I'd have been two weeks younger.

Saffron Well it isn't the end of your life. It may well be only half way through your life, and that's not a prospect I find all that thrilling, believe you me. Try and find something to look forward to, for god's sake.

Edina Oh. And you know a lot about it, do you? Being forty? How often have you ever been forty. Never. This is something that is happening to me and I have to deal with it. You don't know anything about it. It's to do with me. I'm sorry if that seems selfish, but it's me, me, me. It's not your bloody fortieth bloody birthday. *(She takes a swig from the bottle by bed and gets up.)* I need some space. *(She crosses the room.)* I hope you're not organizing anything ... are you? Are you organizing a party or something special for me? I hope not. A special treat or something gorgeous?

Saffron Not if you don't want it. I'd rather not.

Edina What? What have you organized?

Saffron It was going to be a surprise.

Edina No, no, no. Definitely not. You are not to organize a surprise unless I know about it. I will not have a surprise party. If you are organizing something, tell me about it now so I can decide whether or not I want it and what to wear if I do. Only you can't just expect me to go to any old party. I don't want a party. Well, I don't want a huge party with hundreds of my friends, and celebrities, and Japanese finger-food, and a great band, and tequila-slammers all round at midnight.

Saffron Oh, well I'll cancel that then.

Edina *(Desperate.)* No, I would like that, sweetie.

Saffron No.

Edina Oh. *(Pauses.)* What then?

Saffron Look, I didn't know what you'd want, so I've invited people round for a family lunch.

Edina Oh! What do you mean family? I mean, we're hardly the Waltons, are we? Not just you and my mother, I hope.

Saffron Will you stop behaving like this, please?

Edina This *is* how I behave. Anyway I'm allowed to behave however I want on my birthday. Specially to someone who didn't think that I might like a Champagne breakfast. Not even a cup of tea to wake up to on my birthday ... that would have been asking too much.

Saffron Here. *(Hands her a present.)* And don't bother opening it. Throw it straight in the bin, which is probably where you'll put it anyway. *(She gets up and leaves. Edina throws the present in bin.)*

Edina *(Shouting.)* I want a list of who you've invited. And I'm not promising I'll be there. *(She picks up the present and looks at it disdainfully, then begrudgingly rips the paper off and throws the box in the bin. She goes into the bathroom, stands in front of the mirror and flaps her arms.)* Like water wings. I'm sinking into my hips. Faye Dunaway, Morgan Fairchild, Liz Taylor. *(Lets her face drop.)* Larry-bloody-Fortensky. *(She goes back into bedroom and notices the box in the bin.)* 'Lacroix!' Sweetie! *(She opens box and takes out earrings.)*

scene two Edina's Kitchen

Saffron is in the process of clearing away a Champagne breakfast she has laid out for Edina. Edina, in dressing-gown, comes down the stairs wearing the earrings.

Edina Darling. *(Indicates earrings.)* Come to mama, my baby girl. Tell me where you got them? Harvey Nichols?

Saffron and Edina hug.

Saffron Yes.

Edina You should have told me ... I could have got you a discount.

Saffron I'm glad you like them.

Edina Well, they're hardly the normal ill-judged tat that you give me, sweetie ... Lacroix! *(Pauses.)* They are Lacroix, aren't they, sweetie ... not just any old thing you put in the box?

Saffron Do you like them or not?

Edina I like them if they're Lacroix.

Saffron Well, they are.

Edina Good. *(Notices the breakfast.)* Is Patsy here?

Saffron No.

Edina Well, who got that Champagne out?

Saffron I did. For you.

Edina Well, pour me a glass, darling, before it gets warm, for god's sake.

Saffron, barely able to control her temper, goes to open the bottle.

Edina Don't let it pop. Do it gently. *(Comes over all queer.)* Oh, no. Oh, my god. Saffy, darling, help. I'm having a hot flush. I don't believe it. It's a hot flush. Feel my skin.

Saffron You're standing too close to the kettle.

The kettle is boiling in front of Edina.

Edina Oh, god. Thank bloody Christ for that. I thought that was it for me. I thought I was drying up.

Saffron I wish you would. *(Hands her a glass of Champagne.)*

Edina I wonder if I should get some hormone replacement packs here in the house for emergencies. One day you might come home and find a toothless wad of old gum on the floor and have to slap some glands on.

Saffron is starting to prepare lunch.

Edina Who is coming, then?

Saffron So, you're interested?

Edina No, I'm just interested. You're forcing me to ask.

Saffron There's you, me . . . *(Edina sighs.)* Grandma. *(Edina sighs.)* Grandad's staying at home to look after the house.

Edina I thought he was dead. *(She sighs.)*

Saffron Dad ... *(Big sighs from Edina.)* Oliver ... *(Edina now furious.)* Marshall. *(Edina sighs.)*

Edina Overdosing on the ex-husbands, aren't we, darling. I didn't know he was over from LA. How long has he been here? Is my son with him? Is Serge with him?

Saffron No.

Edina Where is Serge? My son, my pride and joy.

Saffron Taking lava samples from a volcano in Hawaii.

Edina Did you invite him?

Saffron I couldn't get hold of him and, yes, I faxed the volcano.

Edina Is that it? Is that the party list then? You, an old woman, two bastard ex-husbands – one with poisonous odious boyfriend.

Saffron And Patsy.

Edina Thank god.

Saffron And you.

Edina Well, I haven't confirmed. *(Pauses.)* What are you doing?

Saffron Making lunch.

Edina *Making* lunch. Cooking?

Saffron Yes.

Edina *Cooking* on our cooker?

Saffron Eventually. Why don't you go upstairs and have a bath while I get on with it. Please.

Edina Don't you need some help?

Saffron Please don't offer. You've only ever used the cooker to light your fags off.

Edina Darling, that is simply not ... *(Thinks.)* ... That is true. But that wasn't what I meant. I meant aren't you using caterers. Why haven't you got caterers? You can't feed people your food.

Saffron I thought it might make a change for you to eat normal food for once.

Edina But I like exotic food. You are what you eat remember, darling.

Saffron Which would make you a large vegetarian tart. Now, please, go and have a bath.

Edina Are you having no one to serve? Why don't you at least get somebody to serve. You could get a Philippino, sweetie. Don't look at me like that – they get paid! They're glad of it. *(She goes to leave, but comes back again.)* You can be a socialist and still have staff, sweetie. *(Mumbling.)* We'll do it all. We can do it ourselves etc. Well, not much of a birthday, so far. You'd think being forty you could expect a bit more, but just a pair of old earrings! And some miserable old family and ex-husbands coming round for lunch. And my son, the one pride and joy of my life, wasn't even contacted. And we're all going to be forced to eat your cooked food and clear away our own plates. Well really ...

Saffron finally snaps and slaps her hard. It is a moment of shock for both of them.

Edina *(Trembling and indignant.)* Did you just slap me then? That's illegal. You're not allowed to hit your parents. Ow! Sweetie.

Saffron Go upstairs. And don't bother coming down again unless you can behave, I'm fed up with it, Mum.

Silence.

ABSOLUTELY fab

Edina I'm sorry, sweetie.

Saffron Not now.

Edina I don't want to go up . . .

Saffron Go.

Edina I like my earrings. *(Begins to leave.)* I'll go and have a bath in them then.

Saffron Thank you.

scene three Edina's Bedroom

Edina is looking out of her window. There is the sound of a bath running. She looks around room and wanders over to her old Buddhist shrine which has some dead flowers and some mouldy fruit around it. She picks up a bell and chants once.

scene four Edina's Kitchen

Saffron is busy preparing lunch. Mother has just entered.

Mother How's it going?

Saffron Fine. I sent Mum up for a bath. Why don't you pop up and see her?

Mother Anything I can do?

Saffron No.

Mother Anything to cut up, or peel?

Saffron No, it's all under control.

Mother Cook?

Saffron No.

Mother Do you want me to wash anything up?

Saffron All done.

Mother Nothing I can help you with? *(She puts a bowl away in cupboard.)*

Saffron I need that bowl.

Mother makes big fuss and bother about taking the bowl out again.

Mother There we are. Not completely useless, you see. Now what else?

There is the sound of a doorbell upstairs.

scene five Edina's Bedroom

Edina hears the doorbell go. She wants to see who it is, goes to bedroom door, then onto the landing and hides behind banisters.

scene six Hallway

Saffron goes to front door and opens it. Marshall and Bo are on the doorstep. Marshall is Edina's first (now ex-) husband. He was a photographer in the Sixties, went to LA to develop a great film script, and has been there ever since developing the same script. He obviously once had a drink and cocaine problem, but is now clean and obsessed with keeping healthy and not drinking. He is nursed through life by Bo, his girlfriend from LA.

Bo Hi!

Saffron Hallo. Come in. Hallo, Marshall.

Bo Hi. I'm Bo. Sweetie, shall we go in?

Marshall Ya.

Bo You must be Saffron.

Marshall Yes, er . . . Saffron. Where's your mother?

As they enter hallway Edina is watching from top of stairs.

Saffron Upstairs. She may be down later.

Bo Maybe I should pop up and say 'hi', give her a hallo hug, tell her I support her and I'm open to her feelings . . . before a whole bunch of people get here.

Marshall and Saffron No.

They all move in the direction of the kitchen. Edina walks back into the bedroom.

Bo Okay. *(Realizing there are steps down to kitchen, babies Marshall down.)* Oh, stairs! Step . . . step . . . step.

scene seven **Edina's Kitchen**
Saffron is getting drinks for Marshall, Bo and Mother.

Saffron Are you sure you wouldn't like to go upstairs to the sitting room?

Bo No, I like the kitchen. It's the hearth, the warm centre of family life. Sit, darling. We like it, don't we, Marshall?

Marshall How is your mother?

Saffron She's well. You know. The same. Bit wider.

Marshall Right. *(To Mother.)* And how are you?

Mother Oh, you know. The same.

Saffron hands Bo a glass of water.

Bo Oh, this is yours, Marshall honey. I see four cubes of ice in it. Is that okay? Shall I put it here for you?

Marshall Ya. Is that a lemon in it?

Bo Is this, may I ask, a lemon in Marshall's water?

Mother Not a whole one?

Bo I think it is, dear.

Marshall Would you take it out for me.

Bo Of course. *(Goes to Saffy.)* Pardon me. Do you have a napkin, or a cloth, or a dish, that I could put this in? Shall I take out some of the ice, too, honey?

Marshall Ya. That would be nice.

Mother Will you cope with just the water, Marshall?

Bo *(To Saffron.)* I'm gonna get rid of a couple of the cubes of ice. The water is really gassy, by the way.

Mother Why don't you have a drink? It's a party. Go on!

Saffron No, Gran.

Bo Please.

Mother Go on. Why don't you just have a little drink? One drink won't kill you. You used to like a drink. Go on, one little drink. Just one tiny sip of a little drink.

Marshall Bo?

Bo Marshall has had an alcohol and drug addiction problem. Don't feel embarrassed. We talk about it really freely. He used to shoot up.

Mother Oh, dear.

She starts to pour out a drink and wafts it very deliberately under Marshall's nose.

Bo Do you want an olive, Marshall? *(Picks up bowl.)* These are black olives and these are green olives. I can take the pips out for you.

The doorbell rings.

scene eight Edina's Bedroom

Edina is wandering around, doing nothing, bored. Hearing the doorbell, she goes onto the landing.

'Champagne, sweetie?'
Almost a catchphrase.

Bubble takes control, or is it just a dream?
BAll three look extraordinarily fabulous.

'**H**orrible,
Horrible,
revolting, devil
children!' Another
fabulous make-up
achievement.

'**F**orty years old.' Yet another fabulous make-up achievement. Jennifer at the time was only thirty-four years old. Give the make-up artist a medal.

Back to their **B**roots. The toilet floor feels like home.

Edina has her finger on the pulse. Looking great in streetwise fashion.

Patsy directs the fashion.

scene nine **Hallway**

Saffron goes to the door. Mother has followed her up.

Saffron I'll do this. You stay with them. Go back and talk to them.

Mother No.

Saffron Please. *(Pauses.)* Do as I tell you.

Mother I'd rather kiss a baboon's bottom, as the saying goes.

Saffron opens the door. It's Justin and Oliver, his boyfriend. Justin is carrying a large box.

Justin Hi, sweetie.

Saffron Dad.

Justin Oliver's here.

Edina is mortally offended.

Saffron Good, I invited you both. Come downstairs. Marshall's here.

Justin I just want you to know that we think this is a very brave thing you are doing. *(Hugs her.)* Whatever happens, sweetie, it's the thought that counts.

Mother It's the thought that stinks.

Justin She's an old woman, what does she know? Not that old can't be beautiful, or not knowing something isn't a positive . . .

They move towards the kitchen. Oliver looks quickly upstairs and sees Edina. Their eyes meet. Edina is very pissed off now. She stays on the landing listening to the sound of Justin and Oliver meeting Marshall and Bo. There is laughter, talking, the clink of glasses, then the sound of a motorbike outside.

scene ten Edina's Bedroom

Edina is standing by the window. There is the sound of a motorbike and Patsy screaming for Eddy. Edina looks out of the window and sees Patsy riding past on the back of a Harley Davidson. They ride past a couple of times, then pull up outside house. Patsy gets off, inelegantly and the biker leaves.

scene eleven Edina's Kitchen

The guests are mingling, chatting, drinking, etc. Justin and Marshall and Oliver are getting on well.

Bo Well, something smells scrummie. What time were you aiming for eating?

Saffron I was aiming for eating two o'clock-ish. I don't have an exact schedule.

Bo Marshall may need to eat soon. He's hyperglycaemic. He gets low energy, and constipation if . . . I don't mash it up.

The door buzzer goes.

Saffron That'll just be Patsy.

Bo takes a crisp, crushes it in her hand, then feeds it to Marshall.

scene twelve Hallway

Patsy enters, picks up an ashtray off the hall table, rips some of the wrapping paper off the present Justin brought and wraps the ashtray up roughly. Edina runs down the stairs to her.

Patsy Happy birthday, Ed. You look great. *(Hands her the present.)* Did you see my ride for the night, Ed?

Edina Thanks, Pats. *(Puts ashtray back on the table.)* Now, Pats. *(Conspiratorially.)* Listen. They're all here.

Patsy Who, darling?

Edina Justin *and* Oliver, Marshall and some bloody LA bimbo.

I mean, at last he's found someone shallow enough to match him.

Patsy Just them. Not much of a party. *(Patsy makes moves to join them.)*

Edina You're not going? *(Pauses.)* No, I *do* want you to go. Go down and see what's happening and talk about me a little. I haven't said I'll come down yet. Look casual. You've come to see me remember, not them. Say that. Then come back upstairs to my room with a bottle.

Patsy Right. See you in a minute, Eddy. What do you want? Champagne?

Edina Yes. Anything that will blur reality.

Patsy exits.

scene thirteen Hallway

It is half an hour later. Edina is sitting on the stairs. Patsy has not returned. She moves towards the door to the kitchen, trying hard to listen. She then gets down on the floor trying to look in. She is trying to look through the bannisters into the kitchen.

scene fourteen Edina's Kitchen

Patsy has joined the party. Everyone is chatting. Patsy is talking to Marshall, who is now fiddling with Chinese worry balls. Bo comes up to him and takes air filter mask out of her bag and asks if he wants to put it on. He waves her away. She makes him wear it round his neck in case. Oliver is talking to Saffron, making her laugh. Mother is talking to Justin.

Mother *(To Justin.)* I want you to look round my house again, Justin. I'm sure there's something I could get on Antiques Roadshow.

Saffron I hope people don't mind eating in the kitchen.

Edina's at the top of the stairs looking through the bannisters trying to attract Patsy's attention. She leans too far forward and plunges headlong down the stairs. Everyone turns to look.

Mother Pay no attention to her. She used to do that as a child.

Saffron laughs. Edina is hurt, but picks herself up with as much dignity as she can muster. Bo rushes up with rescue remedy.

Bo Rescue Remedy! Rescue Remedy!

Edina fights her off, looking at the others.

Edina Get off me ... get off me. I didn't realize a party could have dregs before it had even begun.

Patsy hands her a glass of Champagne.

Patsy Here you are, Eddy.

Edina Just go on having a good time everybody, at my expense. I'm not staying. *(She limps painfully upstairs, with Patsy following.)*

Saffron Are you all right?

Edina I do exist, don't I? You can see me, sweetie. Too late.

Bo I'm sensing a person who's not too happy about what that wee person is feeling right at this moment.

Marshall *(To Oliver.)* Where were we? Oh, yeah, another interesting thing I was going to say was ...

Bo Sweetie, talk to me.

scene fifteen Edina's Bedroom

Edina is sitting on the bed inspecting her legs. Patsy is on the loo.

Edina How can there be so much pain, but not a single mark?

Patsy Hack at them with a razor, sweetie, if you're looking for sympathy.

Edina Maybe I should.

There is a knock at the door.

Saffron Mum? Can I come in?

Edina *(Adopting sad, hurt mode.)* All right, sweetie. As long as you haven't come to hit me again.

Saffron *(Entering.)* Are you okay?

Edina Internal injuries only, darling, if you know what I mean.

Saffron Where's Patsy?

Edina On the loo.

Patsy What?

Saffron *(To Edina.)* Are you coming down?

Patsy What?

Edina We're not talking to you, Pats.

Saffron Are you coming down?

Edina It's always me, isn't it, that has to do everything. I have to go downstairs. I have to get up, get changed, walk downstairs. I don't suppose it occurred to anybody to come up and see me. Oh, no. I've been up here alone for hours being forty. I'll be eighty years old and dribbling into my incontinence pads before you visit me up here. All on my own. Being forty, all on my own.

Patsy *(Entering.)* Can I borrow some tights and knickers? I didn't get home last night.

Edina They're in here. Second drawer.

Saffron Please come down. We're about to eat.

Edina Hardly the high point ... Hardly a tempting smorgasbord waiting downstairs. I suppose you invited Oliver just to spite me.

Saffron He's Dad's boyfriend. It's right he should be here.

Edina It's *my* birthday.

Saffron Why do you hate him?

Edina Oh, god.

Saffron What's the real reason? It's not because he's gay.

Edina Please, sweetie, I'd come to terms with that fact of life before they had. All my friends are gay.

Saffron Then why?

Pause.

Edina Why is it taking you so long to find a pair of knickers, Pats?

Patsy Have you got any G-string or are they all jumbo?

Edina I think there's an old pair of G-strings there. Not that I've worn them for a few years. Not since I caught sight of my backview trying something on in Harvey Nic's, and thought I was sharing the cubicle with a sumo wrestler.

Edina looks back to Saffy. There is a pause. Edina is waiting for Saffron to speak.

Saffron Well?

Edina Oh, it's my pause, is it? What have I got to say?

Saffron Why you hate Oliver?

Edina Darling, I thought it was perfectly obvious. I hate him because you like him. I saw you down there, chatting and joking and laughing with him. Oh, very nice. Oh, ha-ha-ha. I have to plunge headlong down a vertical staircase and suffer unspeakable pain to even raise a reluctant smile.

Saffron I promise I won't talk to Oliver if you come downstairs.

Edina Oh, all right.

ABSOLUTELY fab

Saffron Just try and relax and enjoy yourself.

Edina I'll be very, very, very good.

Saffron *(Gets up to go and passes Patsy.)* I think you'll find they've all got crotches.

scene sixteen Edina's Kitchen

Everybody, including Patsy and Edina, is sitting around the table. Edina is dressed very demurely in black. They are eating the starter, a vegetarian mousse. There is a slightly tense atmosphere.

Mother Not eating, Patsy?

Patsy Liquid lunch for me, Mrs M.

Mother No wonder you're still thin as a rake. Gentlemen like something to grab hold of. Isn't that right, Oliver?

Oliver looks embarrassed.

Bo *(To Patsy.)* You have a terrific figure.

Edina *(Taking the piss.)* What a sweet thing to say. Gee, whiz, isn't she the cutest thing!

Saffron Mum.

Edina Darling, I'm being nice. Where did you find her, Marshall? Floating around LA with the rest of the airheads. But then you've been through a few in the last fifteen years.

Saffron Mum, don't, you promised.

Edina Well, we've got to do something to take our minds off the food.

Justin *(To Marshall.)* How's the script coming, Marshall?

Edina Are we talking about the same script that you've been developing for the past fifteen years?

Marshall It's at a really exciting stage.

Bo Yes, Marshall has recently signed a new development deal with Paramount. It's at a very exciting stage.

Edina *(To Saffron.)* I'll just clear these up on my birthday. I'll be my own servant on my own birthday, shall I?

Saffron I'll do it. *(Saffron starts to scrape left-overs onto other plates.)*

Edina Can you not do that in front of me, or I'll throw up. Are you all right, Pats?

Patsy is talking to Oliver.

Edina You can squash up here if you want?

Patsy I'm okay, darling.

Justin Weren't Al Pacino and Anjelica Houston going to be in it?

Bo Well, I think you kind of took a different, refreshing course, didn't you, darling?

Marshall Yes, the Anjelica part is going to be played by a dog.

Bo Not just any dog.

Marshall The dog from *Down and Out in Beverly Hills*.

Bo Even getting that dog to look at a contract is impossible. Is your water okay, Marshall?

Patsy So Al Pacino and a dog.

Bo Well . . . you tell 'em, honey.

Marshall We went off the idea of the dog having a friend.

Justin *(Laughing.)* Just the dog.

Bo *Home Alone*, but it's a pooch. I think it's cute. Do you need antacid, Marsh, sweetheart?

Marshall No. I mean, what would your pet dog do, if you left him at home on his own?

Bo Funny or what?

Mother 'What' ... from where I'm sitting.

Marshall suddenly chokes, and Bo jumps up and shouts.

Bo Heimlich manoeuvre ... Heimlich manoeuvre, I'm trained in this. *(She performs the manoeuvre and nearly kills him.)*

Edina What do we do now we've cleared away those plates?

Saffron Just sit down.

Edina No, I want to work on my birthday. *(Picks up a carving knife.)* Isn't there something I could cut up. *(She walks behind Bo and mimes cutting her throat. Mother nods.)*

Bo *(To Oliver.)* You're in antiques, as well?

Oliver Yes, Justin and I have a shop.

Edina Shop? It's not what I'd call a shop. A few miserable old bits of furniture. You have to ring a bell before they let you in, and then you're lucky. Unwelcoming? Vincent Price could take lessons.

Bo How do they make furniture look so old?

Oliver Just let it live with Edina for a few years. That usually ages it.

Bo I love old things. They make me feel very centred, very warm. It must be very satisfying handling antiques.

Oliver He should know. *(Indicating Justin.)* He was married to one.

Edina Anything old or secondhand you deal in, don't you. Can't keep your hands off secondhand goods ...

Patsy Touché. Cheers, Eddy.

Bo I'm sensing aggression here.

Oliver looks to Justin for a reaction.

Oliver *(To Justin.)* Are you just going to sit there and let me take this?

Justin I'll handle it.

Saffron Mum. Go upstairs.

Justin No, I'll deal with this. Gee, whiz. You're a bad woman.

Oliver I think we should go. I can see nothing to celebrate in the fact that she has lived so long. If you're not coming now, you can contact me at the YMCA.

Saffron *(To Edina.)* I hope you're happy.

Edina Warming up, sweetie. One down...

scene seventeen Downstairs Toilet

Edina and Patsy are smoking a joint in the loo.

Edina Do you feel your age?

Patsy Not really. And I make a point of not acting it.

Edina All these things have happened to me ... My life has been lived and I don't know how. I've got two ex-husbands and a child sitting downstairs, and this house, and all these things, and I don't really know where they all came from. Don't know if I want them. I want to be at home with my record-player and my posters, and ... not wearing any makeup without frightening people. I came home from a party the other night, believing I had looked so 'cool', feeling great. I had been Kathleen Turner, I had flirted seductively, I had been funny and loud and gorgeous. I came home on such a high and then I looked in the mirror, and felt entirely annihilated. My hair had gone flat and parted itself in the middle, my lipstick had

disappeared entirely. I looked like a two-hundred-year-old dying red indian dwarf!

Patsy You had fun. Who gives a shit, darling.

Edina And that's another thing. When did we start calling people 'darling'? I can remember finding it impossible. It was a word your parents used for each other. I could say 'man' and 'babe', but not 'darling'. And now I can't stop saying it. Darling, darling, darling, darling, darling, darling, darling, darling...

Patsy Oh shut up, Eddy.

scene eighteen Edina's Kitchen

Saffron and Justin are putting candles on a birthday cake.

Saffron Hand me some more candles, Dad.

Justin This is a bad idea ... forty candles.

Bo She's not coping with this forty thing, is she? I mean, golly, I wish I could tell her that it's no big deal. I had a ball on my fortieth birthday. I felt really strong ... really sorted out about it. I realized what a wonderful lucky person I was and whether you're in your thirties, or your forties you're the same gorgeous person. Enjoy your life!

Mother When will you be fifty?

Bo acts as though she has been punched in the stomach – begins choking and having difficulty breathing. She starts singing 'I feel pretty ...' and dancing round room.

Marshall She hasn't started fifty therapy yet.

scene nineteen Toilet

Edina I hate Morgan-Bloody-Fairchild.

Patsy I hate Jane-Bloody-Fonda.

Edina I hope all their old skin comes back to haunt them.

Patsy I bought that bloody woman's tapes. I paid for those plastic domes on her chest. I want them when she dies.

Edina Even after she dies, she'll still be squeezing her buns.

Patsy Feeling them burn in hell, I hope.

Edina There must be a moment about a week after death when all those women finally achieve the figure they desire.

Patsy Skeleton-thin with plastic bumps.

Edina And when all the flesh has rotted from their bones, the bumps will still be there. Little coffins filled with bones and bumps.

scene twenty Edina's Kitchen

They are all finishing off the main course.

Bo Is it mashed up enough for you, honey? I could liquidize that last little bit, if you like.

Marshall No, it was nice.

Bo Have a little drink now.

Justin *(To Saffron.)* Have you kept some for your mother?

Saffron No.

Justin Good girl.

Bo May I have a little quality moment here. May I? Can I just stop here and say I think it is . . . Can we hold hands?

Mother Oh, please no.

Bo Come on. Everybody. Just for a moment.

They all awkwardly hold hands round the table.

Bo Let us be thankful for this day that has brought us all together.

Marshall That's enough now, Bo. We know why we're here.

Mother Duty.

Justin I'm here because of my daughter.

Bo Well. There must be more. I mean, you were both married to her. Obviously it was an error on Marshall's part. He was weak.

She moves to help Saffron.

Justin He was stoned.

Marshall It was the worst trip of my life.

Mother Why you ever married her, Justin, I don't know.

Saffron Gran!

Justin Well, I had ... *(Looks at Saffron.)*. I ... er ... she was. It seemed a good idea at the time. She was going through a bad patch.

Marshall *(Leaning forward to Justin.)* At least, you got away without being sucked dry. I'm paying her child support for a child I'm supporting. How do you like that?

Justin I'm paying.

Bo *(Overhearing.)* How much?

Marshall Let me handle this, Bo.

Bo Well, get to the point, honey.

Justin She told me she got nothing from you.

Marshall and Bo Nothing! Nothing!

Bo Marshall is paying.

Marshall Okay, Bo.

Justin God damn!

Saffron What is it, Dad?

Justin Nothing. *(Barely controlling his temper.)* I've just got to go upstairs a minute, sweetness. I'm okay. *(He exits.)*

Bo *(To Marshall.)* Ask him again. Get it in writing.

scene twenty-one Edina's Bedroom

Justin enters and starts smashing things up in a fit of hatred.

scene twenty-two Downstairs Toilet

Patsy and Edina put out joint, and put on lipstick, etc. They are both stoned.

Patsy I know, Marsh is brain-dead, but that woman . . .

Edina The vacuum was so strong in her head, she's sucked out all Marsh's brain cell into her skull, that's why.

They both laugh.

Edina She does all his talking for him.

Patsy Oh, that is a weird thought.

There is a knock on door. It is Mother.

Patsy It's no-smoking day today. Bloody no-smoking day.

Edina They don't have a nobody-can-be-a-boring-old-fart day.

Patsy Or nobody-can-wear-bloody-awful-clothes day . . .

Mother It's Mother. Saffron wants to know, are you going to be long in there burning joss sticks . . . As if I don't know.

Edina *(Laughing.)* We're coming.

Mother Sounds like more fun in there, dear. *(She returns to the party.)*

Edina Look at me. I'm forty years old. I'm fed up with being good on my birthday.

Patsy You've done your best.

Edina All sweetness and light. I know. Well, sometimes, I've just got to be me.

scene twenty-three Edina's Kitchen

Edina and Patsy return. They have changed. Oliver has gone. All the others are standing around a candle-lit birthday cake.

Mother Oh, here she comes.

Everybody starts singing happy birthday, and Edina sprays all the candles out with a fire extinguisher.

Bo *(To Edina, as she approaches her intimately.)* Can I just say ... 'every life is more or less a trash can among whose garbage we have to look out what the person ought to have been'.

Patsy I'm gonna deal with her.

Edina It's okay, I've got it.

Bo Soak it in, like a sponge. Let it permeate. In as anger, out as love.

Edina *(To Justin.)* What are you still here for?

Justin I ... er ... I have to give you your present.

Edina Presents! Oh, yes, presents. It's my birthday. I get presents. Already I've had a gorgeous, gorgeous pair of earrings from my darling daughter, which I'm wearing. *(She notices that one has dropped off.)*

Patsy Down the toilet, Eds.

Edina And a gorgeous thing from Pats. So, Marsh, baby, where's my present?

Marshall (*Looks to Bo.*) Sweetheart?

Bo I have the gift. (*She hands it to Edina.*)

Edina (*Opening it.*) What the buggery-bollocks is this?

Bo It's a copy . . . a signed copy of my book on ancient oils.

Edina throws it towards the bin.

Edina Next!

Bo Marshall, don't you find that very insulting?

Marshall I've lived with her. Believe me, this is flirtation.

Bo sits down in shock. Mother has taken a ring-side seat, Saffron is clearing up.

Edina Now, where's my next present?

Justin In the hall.

Edina It's not a horrid little piece of furniture, is it? It's in the hall, Pats. Let's check it out.

Mother (*To Saffron.*) Well done, dear. It's been a perfect day for her.

Justin Her idea of fun . . . a bit of blood sport.

Mother I don't mind her using those two as target practice.

Bo We'll get back to talking about money later on. She can't need much. She's got a tiny little daughter to feed.

scene twenty-four Living Room

Patsy and Edina are karaoking Sixties numbers. Justin is looking on with Saffron.

Justin I guess it's just what she always wanted.

Edina is blowing kisses to him.

Edina I've had an absolutely fabulous birthday.

scene twenty-five Living Room

It is much later on. Edina and Patsy are singing along very seriously to Julie Driscoll's 'Wheels on Fire'. Bo and Marshall are sitting on the couch. Marshall is asleep. Bo is putting an oxygen mask to his face occasionally. Mother is asleep. Justin is awake and tapping his foot along to the music. Marshall wakes and says 'a funny rabbit!'. Saffron watches as Edina gets more and more involved in the song.

Bo I've been doing an inventory of this house . . . and that little girl doesn't need much. It's just the two of them living in this big house.

Scene fades out.

magazine

Cast List

Edina · JENNIFER SAUNDERS

Patsy · JOANNA LUMLEY

Saffron · JULIA SAWALHA

Mother · JUNE WHITFIELD

Patsy's Mother · ELEANOR BRON

Kathy · DAWN FRENCH

Hamish · ADRIAN EDMONDSON

Catriona · HELEN LEDERER

Fleur · HARRIET THORPE

Magda · KATHY BURKE

scene one Hallway

It is very early morning and dark apart from the street light through window. There is the sound of someone trying the front door. Eventually it opens, and a figure walks in, setting off a burglar alarm. Figure goes to a flashing panel and tries to punch in numbers. Nothing works. Figure hits it, and alarm changes to a loud siren. The lights go on. Saffron appears at top of the stairs, then goes to panel and switches the alarm off.

Saffron Nought ... nought ... nought ... Enter.

The figure is Edina, looking somewhat worse for wear.

Edina Stupid, bloody thing.

Saffron We made it the simplest number possible, so that even a fool could remember it. Over-estimated you again.

Edina I don't know why we need the bloody thing. It makes such a bloody racket.

Saffron It's supposed to.

Edina What's the point of it if it's only there to wake me up? I don't care if someone takes the furniture. I can get the furniture back on the insurance. But I can't get my sleep back. I can't put on the claim form, six hours' sleep.

Saffron I'll have to go and ring the central station and let them know it was a false alarm. And then I need to speak to you. *(She exits to kitchen.)*

Edina Oh! Speak to me? I'm shaking in my boots, sweetie.

Patsy appears in dressing-gown at top of stairs.

Patsy What? What is it?

Edina Just me.

Patsy Have you just come in?

Edina Oh, yes, just. Just this moment come into my own house. After a rather gorgeous night. La–la–la. Go back to bed, Pats.

Patsy What time is it?

Edina Seven–thirty.

Patsy What? In the . . . er . . . Seven–thirty, you say . . . That means nothing to me.

Edina Go back to bed.

Edina exits to the kitchen, leaving Patsy looking confused and slightly dejected.

scene two Edina's Kitchen

Saffron is standing, looking very strict. Edina is facing her.

Saffron What are you smirking at? Do you think this is funny?

Edina *(In a strangely silly mood.)* Think what? Funny what? Ha, ha, ha.

Saffron You might have rung and let me know what you were doing.

Edina I was too busy doing it, sweetie. What's the matter? Jealous?

Saffron No. Worried.

Edina Worried I might be having some fun? Well, I was! Bloody great, bloody fun.

Patsy *(Entering.)* Ask her who with?

Saffron Who with?

Edina Jean-Pierre.

Patsy Not that bastard. You didn't tell me he was around.

Edina I met him by accident. We had a great time. *(Starts singing* *a bit of rap.)* He's over directing a new video. Really hip, rave, great rap band.

Patsy *(Grabbing a bottle of brandy.)* I thought we were going out, Eds. Thanks to you, I had to spend a whole evening alone in the same house as . . . Helena Bonham Carter . . . here. Well, I'm going back to bed. No point in me being up at this hour. *(Indicates bottle.)* Help me sleep.

Saffron What, is the light hurting you? Get back in your coffin.

Edina Patsy is an insomniac!

Saffron More like the walking dead.

Patsy exits. Edina is rapping away.

Saffron How long is she living here for?

Edina I don't know. How long are you here for?

Saffron She's your friend. You should be responsible enough to come home and entertain her. I won't do it again.

Edina What do you mean entertain her, sweetie? What did you do? Play charades, sing around the piano, recite some old school poems, or play Botti-bloody-celli. Poor Pats.

Saffron How long?

Edina Until her flat has been fumigated. She can't live in it, breathing fumes all day.

Saffron Why not? I thought sniffing chemicals was what she did best. I'm surprised she's not out there with a straw up her nose already. She should try it. It might actually be the one substance that makes her socially acceptable.

Edina It would kill her.

Saffron Exactly . . . so Jean-Pierre.

Edina Yup . . . La, la, la.

Saffron Is he over for long?

Edina I think that depends on me. He sort of made it quite clear last night, darling, that he was fairly well, re-smitten, if you know what I mean.

Saffron Did you . . . ?

Edina Oh, yes. I know it's been a while, but it's a bit like riding a bike. You never forget.

Saffron I hope . . .

Edina Very careful. Whole packet, darling. Once we'd have brushed away the cobwebs, there was no stopping us.

Saffron Mum!

Edina You asked the question. No point getting prudish now, for god's sake. Anything else you'd like to know, darling?

Saffron No.

Edina I mean, if you maybe had a few more boyfriends yourself you might not be so hung up about the whole issue.

Saffron I am not hung up.

Edina I know it's a sensitive issue with someone your age and you must develop in your own time. Bit embarrassed about the whole thing, but Jesus Christ! Not one boyfriend in the whole time that I have known you. What's the matter with you? You're not that ugly. Have you read the Karma Sutra I gave you? No! The dutch cap I gave you has only ever seen the light of day. Here I am, your mother, waiting poised for your first sexual experience but night after night dry sheets. I don't want a little moustached virgin for a daughter, so please do something about it?

Silence.

Edina Unless of course . . .

Saffron Please don't . . .

Edina Darling, unless of course you're . . .

Saffron Don't, Mum.

Edina Unless, of course, you're gay.

Saffron Mum!

Edina Well? Darling? Are you? You can tell me.

Saffron All right . . . yes, I'm gay.

Edina Oh, sweetie, hurrah. Well done, darling! *(She hugs her.)*

Saffron I'm glad it makes you happy, but . . . actually, I'm not.

Edina What?

Saffron I'm not gay.

Edina Oh. *(Disappointed.)*

Saffron I'm sorry.

Edina Break it to me, like that. Oh, it's not your fault, darling. Just your old mother clutching at straws. Trying to find one interesting, exotic feature. Never mind. Oh, well, what's the time?

Saffron Eight-ish.

Edina Wake me at nine-thirty. Let the world warm up a bit, have its first fag.

Saffron It's normally smoked twelve packets and been diagnosed as having lung cancer by the time you hit the road.

Edina exits.

scene three Edina's Kitchen

It is mid-morning. Patsy is up, dressed and sitting at the table drinking strong black coffee. Saffron is reading a paper. Patsy lights a fag, takes deep drag and starts to cough her guts up.

ABSoluTELy fa

Saffron All night I've had to hear that. Any more hacking and you'll bring up oil.

Edina enters down the stairs. She is dressed rather nicely.

Edina Has anyone called?

Saffron No. What are you wearing?

Edina Is it awful? I'm seeing Jean-Pierre for lunch, Pats. I thought it was, sort of him.

Patsy It is him, darling . . . but it is not you.

Edina Saff?

Saffron I like it.

Edina I'll change!

Patsy Did you say you were seeing him for lunch?

Edina Yes, Pont de la Tour.

Patsy I thought *we* were having lunch.

Edina I always have lunch with you, Pats.

Patsy Can't I come?

Edina You don't like Jean-Pierre.

Patsy Nobody likes Jean-Pierre. I wouldn't talk to him. I'd talk to you. I just don't want you to make a horrible mistake again.

Edina What do you mean?

Patsy Listen, darling, I'm your best friend and, let's be honest, your taste in men is famously bad. I've had to save you from two disastrous marriages and some ghastly pathetic affairs you might nearly have had.

Saffron What a great friend you are, Patsy!

Patsy Don't make me have lunch on my own.

Edina You can get someone to have lunch with.

Patsy Of course, I can *get* someone. I can always get someone. It's just . . . I haven't *got* someone. Go on.

Edina Oh, all right, you can come.

A look passes between Saffron and Patsy.

Patsy Thanks, Eddy. Are you going into your office?

Edina Well, there are a few things I need to sort out about the shop. *(She stands up.)* It's all looking very exciting. I've got great pots and things coming in from Kashmir, Afghanistan, Albania, and blankets and rugs from Ethiopia, dirt cheap. I got a load of those lip plates from dead Amazonian Indians, that I thought could be ashtrays. *(To Saffron.)* Don't look at me like that, we can take the lips off. Lots of kitchen pots and pans from Somalia. They don't need them, they've got no food to eat off them. But, best news of all, you know all those villages that were deserted by the Kurds . . . *I've* got that franchise.

Patsy Well done, Eddy!

Edina Trucks are moving in as we speak.

Saffron Coups, revolutions, disasters . . . They're all bargain basements to you.

Edina Darling, they're happy camping. Pats, what are you up to today?

Saffron She's not lolling around the house again.

Edina Will you shut up. I'm not talking to you. I'm talking to my friend. It's like living with a chronically-depressed budgerigar, living with you sometimes.

Patsy I've got to go into the office!

Edina and Saffron are shocked into silence.

Edina Sorry, sweetie? Your . . .

Patsy Office.

Edina At the magazine? Is it still there?

Patsy Of course. There's a little meeting I've got to go to. Ten minutes at the most.

Saffron What do you do?

Edina and Patsy are both shocked.

Edina Darling, Patsy is one of the country's top fashion editors on a major magazine.

Patsy Director. Executive Fashion Director.

Saffron But she's never at work.

Patsy I am always at work.

Edina Thanks to our wonderful friend, the mobile telephone. Anyway, Pats has got that job for life.

Saffron You don't mean to say she's actually good at something.

Edina No, darling. She slept with the publisher.

Patsy And I'm bloody good at it.

Edina Of course, you are.

Saffron What does a fashion director do?

Edina Darling, she drinks free Champagne, gets free merchandizing and free clothes. She commands her own booth in most good restaurants and has a fifty per cent discount at Harvey Nic's. I mean, if it wasn't for Patsy I'd hardly be able to afford to eat and dress in quite the style I manage now.

Patsy It's not just that. I mean there is work involved. Skill.

Edina Of course, there is.

Patsy I decide what goes in the magazine. One snap of my fingers and I can raise hem-lines so high that the world is your gynaecologist.

Patsy I . . . direct.

Edina The fashion.

Saffron Lots more free things?

Edina Yes.

Saffron You two have never had to pay for anything, have you?

Edina Don't worry, sweetie, I've paid for you.

Patsy A hundred times over.

Edina I'll change quickly, then we'll go.

Patsy I'm still coming to lunch?

Edina Yes.

Edina exits.

Saffron How sad! You're so afraid if Mum has a boyfriend it'll make you look like a lonely, pathetic old cow.

Patsy hisses at her and exits.

scene four Outside Patsy's Magazine Building

Patsy and Edina pull up in back of car, and get out.

Patsy I'm sure this is the one. They've cleaned the outside, or something . . . That's why I was confused.

Edina *(To driver.)* Wait here. I won't be long.

Patsy and Edina enter the building.

Patsy Now . . .

Edina Third floor, isn't it? *(To receptionist.)* Can you tell me where the lifts are?

Patsy I think I moved.

Patsy and Edina walk along, confused. Edina is holding a list. People are coming in and out of offices and Patsy smiles at a few of them as if she might know them — she's not sure.

Edina *(Looking at list.)* I can't see you down here. Editor. Deputy Editor. Beauty Editor. Chief-Sub Editor. Fashion Editor. Health and Beauty Editor. Travel Editor. Literary Editor. Insight and Design Editor. Food and Drink Editor. Deputy and Features Editor. Managing Editor. Assistant Editor. Friend of Editor. Copy Deputy Editor. Chief-Sub Editor. Senior Sub Editor. Sub Editor. Social Editor. Interiors Editor. Picture Editor. Assistant Retail Markets Editor. Special Projects Editor.

Patsy Are you looking at the list of editors?

Edina Yes.

Patsy I'm a Fashion Director.

Edina Right. Here we go. *(She reads.)* Arts Director. Style Director. Circulation Director. Managing Director. Ad Director. Promotions Director . . .

scene five **Patsy's Office**

The office is much as Patsy left it — not very tidy. Items of clothing, cigarette stubs in ashtray, large wardrobe unit to one side filled with free samples of clothing, tights, makeup, etc. Huge bunches of flowers around, some dying, some fresh. Opened bottle of Champagne on desk with glasses. There are some unvased bunches of flowers on desk. Edina and Patsy enter.

Patsy This is it.

Edina As you left it, by the look of things. Now, let's not be long.

Patsy *(Looks through bunches of flowers. Selects some, chucks one bunch directly in the bin.)* Nobody gets flowers from that florist any more. Bloody cheek. *(Looks at label of another bunch.)* Oh, Gucci. Only the second time I've been bunched by them. About bloody time.

Edina *(Looking at cupboard.)* Is this the samples?

Patsy Help yourself.

Edina rifles through clothes and products. She finds a blazer she likes.

Edina Oh, nice. Look, Armani. *(The name is written on the sleeve.)*

Patsy Only Emporio.

Edina Darling, I can felt-pen that bit out.

Patsy has opened Champagne – she pours.

Patsy Is my Chanel still in there?

Edina *(Produces Chanel suit on hanger.)* This one?

Patsy Yes, my little baby. I think I'll put it on if there's a meeting. It frightens the editors. I'm the only one with Chanel couture. Let them kiss my buttons.

Magda the editor enters.

Magda Patsy Stone.

Patsy Hallo, Mag. You know Eddy.

Magda Yeah. Look are you coming to this meeting?

Patsy If I must.

Magda Good. We need to drum up some more advertising revenue. It's not looking good this month. We've lost Swiss Watches, Nivea, Lanson, two lingeries, one showergel, and all my tampons have dropped out.

Edina Oh, dear.

Magda If it wasn't for a three-page Estee Lauder and bloody Rive Gauche, we'd be looking pretty thin this month.

Edina It won't be long this meeting, will it?

Magda Five mins at the most. I've got three lunches and a tights launch to get to by two o'clock. And this, with my late-working breakfast with Marie Helvin still floating about here. *(Indicates top of her stomach.)* I'll see you there in two minutes. *(She exits.)*

Patsy All right. Chuck me the Chanel, Eds.

scene six Small Conference Room

Sitting around a table sipping Champagne are Patsy, Edina, Catriona (Feature Editor), Fleur (Beauty Editor). There are lots of pots of cosmetics, etc., on table all being tried. There are also some shoes, watches, bits of jewellery being tried on, and copies of Vogue, Harpers, Elle, *etc., which they are bitching about.*

148 | 149

Fleur *(To Patsy.)* Did you go to the opening of Katherine's new shop?

Patsy I went, yes. Cheap wine and crap canapés. Unless I get my discount card pretty quick, she'll find herself plunged into obscurity designing for British Home Stores. Where's Magda?

Catriona On the phone to Fergie.

Magda enters.

Magda Right! I've got one minute. Just run through what you're thinking about for this month. Okay, Features. Catriona.

Catriona Well...

Magda Do something about a car.

Catriona What?

Magda Do something about a car. A nice one. I need a new car. No rubbish.

Catriona Right.

Magda And something about how lovely Champagne is.

Catriona Right. Well, maybe I could tie that in with a thing on glasses. A friend of mine has a shop with some lovely glasses.

Fleur Henrietta?

Catriona Yes. We could do some lovely photos.

Magda What about people? Who's in, who's out? Who's sexy, who's not sexy? Who's clever, who's not clever?

Catriona Who's in, who's out?

Magda Here's my list. Oh, hang on, she's out, she screwed me. Oh, and he's in, he screwed me. Oh, and do something on River Phoenix. I fancy him.

Catriona Right.

Magda River Phoenix, Mickey Rourke, and Liam Neeson. I don't like anyone called Freud. Put that in. Bunch of no-talents with an ancestor.

Catriona But they were in last month.

Magda So! I'm not running a charity. Just because some old grandad came up with penis envy, doesn't mean I have to lick their boots.

Catriona Yeah, right. It's just that they're really good friends of mine, but it doesn't matter.

Magda Right. Beauty and make it quick.

Patsy (*To Eddy.*) She's fabulous!

Edina Puts you into perspective, babe.

Fleur Clarins, Shisheido, Paloma Picasso, Chanel, makeup, Germolene, lipsticks, powder bases, faces, eyes, lips, nostrils. This is all off the top of my head. Douching with mint is a thought. Ten tips for tropical toenails. I'm thinking natural zing. 'Moist' is my word de jour. Skin is in. Lovely moist wet lips. Wet droplets. Sun, sea, sand, water, waves, beach. I see a photo shoot. I'm looking at two weeks in the Caribbean. And the usual – try and be more beautiful if you want to have more sex.

Magda Good. Chuck us that wrinkle cream. *(Presses button on intercom.)* Get Hamish in here. I need to know about the restaurant I'm having lunch at. Patsy?

Patsy Only big names, this month. Lauren, Armani, Lagerfeld, Montana, Oscar de la Renta, in Moscow. Glamour in Red Square.

Magda Not using Russians.

Patsy No, all too bloody ugly. Four-hundred years on a potato diet ain't gonna fit into a Gautier cup.

Magda If I looked like that, I wouldn't go out.

Hamish, the Food and Drink Editor, enters.

Hamish Magda?

Magda What's that new French place like?

Hamish Well? Competent in the grand manner, stuffed with plutocratic goodies and a decent duck. A boudoiresque dining room, fin-de-siecle eclectic and still fashionably uncomfortable. A melange, possibly a post-Orwellian version of an Edwardian eaterie. The food ecumenical in flavour, a cosmopolitan adventure of exuberant eclecticism full of amuse gueles and gastro-credibility. No flash in the bain-marie this. It has a comforting ambience, although generally the tomatoes were rather 'pulpeuse'.

Magda Ta!

Hamish exits.

Magda Load of bollocks, but it uses up paper and that's what magazines are about. Before I go, Patsy, one little thing. The television have been on to us – need someone to do a fashion makeover for breakfast television, tomorrow morning. Their regular dropped out. Good for the magazine, so I said you'd do it.

Patsy Are you mad?

Magda My secretary has the details. There's a couple of miseries in shell-suits, sitting downstairs, waiting for you to perform a miracle on them. *(She exits.)*

Patsy Help me, Eddy.

Edina I'm going to lunch.

Patsy What do I do?

Edina You take them out, get them a haircut, put them in designer, then parade them on television. Public humiliation . . . Nothing you can't handle.

Patsy Television? I go on television?

Edina Yes.

Patsy *(Suddenly keen on the idea.)* Oh! Me on television. I've always thought I'd be rather good at that.

Edina I'll see you later.

Patsy On television. Will you be in this evening?

Edina Probably. I don't know. You'll be all right.

Patsy Oh, yes. Piece of cake. See you later, Eddy. I'm going to convert my shell-suits to Montana and Oscar de la Renta. *(As Edina exits, she practises talking to TV camera.)* 'Hi, I'm Patsy Stone'.

scene seven Edina's Kitchen

Saffron comes downstairs and fixes herself a drink. We hear Patsy come in upstairs.

Patsy Eddy! Eddy! *(Sees Saffron.)* Jesus Christ.

Saffron She's not in. How did the makeover go?

Patsy *(Going straight to fridge for a drink.)* How do you know about that?

Saffron Mum phoned. She's not back till later. Out on her own with Jean-Pierre, having a great time, without you. So, have you managed to turn some normal happy people into pathetic fashion freaks this afternoon?

Patsy Bitches! They had no taste. We disagreed. The whole thing is off.

Saffron Oh.

Patsy It was hideous.

Saffron The outfit?

Patsy The fight. The repellent mother and I came to blows over a geometric bob. I told her the only thing she looked good in was a body bag. And the daughter rebelled in Yamihotos shop. She is now in hospital having a piece of modern furniture removed from her. Filthy little slut. No thought for me and my reputation, and the fact that I've got to be on television tomorrow morning. Two fantastic outfits and nobody to fill them. Selfish peasants.

Saffron I'm weeping.

Saffron exits. Patsy is left alone in kitchen, a thought slowly dawning on her.

scene eight Saffron's Bedroom

A cosy room with simple bed, desk, sensible posters, bookshelves. Saffron is listening to some classical music. There is a knock at the door.

Saffron Don't bother.

Patsy Can I come in?

Saffron I know what you want and the answer is 'no'.

Patsy opens the door and enters, with bottle and two glasses.

Patsy How can you know what I want?

Saffron Well, maybe, I'm wrong. I thought you'd come up here to persuade me to be a fashion victim for you, but perhaps you've come for a little chat, a cosy little personal little chat with me, Patsy. *(She goes to shut door.)*

Patsy Don't shut that door.

Saffron Don't you like my room?

Patsy Well, it's as I expected. A cell ... curtains.

Saffron Would you mind dragging your old carcass out of here ... now.

Patsy I'm sorry. Look. *(Laughs falsely.)* I know I pretend to hate you, and you pretend to hate me.

Saffron I *do* hate you.

Patsy Why?

Saffron You're a despicable person who has resented me since the day I was born.

Patsy Before.

Saffron So, why should I ever do you a favour?

Patsy I'll pay you.

Saffron No.

Patsy I'm your mother's best friend.

Saffron Best friend! What kind of friend are you?

Patsy What kind of daughter are you? At least, she has fun with me.

Saffron I care about her.

Patsy Care about her! You may dress like a Christian, but the similarity ends there. I think you do it on purpose. How long does it take you to get the crease so crisp down the front of your jeans? You torturer.

Saffron Get out.

Patsy Look, I understand.

Saffron You don't understand anything. Get out.

Patsy We have a lot more in common than you know.

Saffron I hope not.

Patsy At least your mother wanted you, and despite everything, and believe me I've tried to dissuade her from this, she loves you.

Saffron If this is going to be one of your terrible sob stories, make it quick, I can barely hold back the tears. Go on, tell me about your tragic childhood. About these parents of yours that we never hear anything from, who you've probably had committed to an old people's home to get them out of your way.

Patsy They're dead. Smirk your way out of that one, babe.

Saffron I'm sorry.

Patsy has got her.

Patsy Yes, well. I never knew my father . . . my mother only knew him fairly briefly. She had me when she was in her forties.

I nursed her through her last years. It sort of put a stopper on me finding someone for myself and settling down, but, there you are, it wasn't her fault. She didn't want a child and would have got rid of me, but mistook being pregnant for the menopause . . . and when she found out it was too late.

Saffron Patsy, that's awful.

Patsy It was having Eddy and your grandmother that made it okay. Gave me somewhere to go. I couldn't really stay in the house with my mother. I cramped her style . . . made her feel old.

Scene fades into flashback.

scene nine Flashback to 1964

Living room in Patsy's mother's house.

Patsy is fourteen years old. She and her mother live in a large rambling, very bohemian house. Her mother is a mad, bohemian woman, a writer, early feminist cross-between Germaine Greer and Isadora Duncan.
The living room is lit from large windows. It is full of smoke from joss sticks, and lots of Marrakech furnishing. There is the sound of Wagner music. The walls are lined with books. A door bursts open, and mother enters.

Patsy's mother I am Aphrodite. *(She swirls across the room.)* I live. I breathe. I am Diana, Queen Dido. Oh, what a light dances over the world. *(She suddenly notices Patsy.)* Get out of my way, child. Don't stand in my path when I'm trying to express . . . What are you doing here? They cut the cord when you were born, when my body expelled you. Accept your liberty, my little void, and let this spirit be free. Anyway, I've got Humphrey and Andre coming over. I would rather not have you around. If you're planning to go out, don't forget the key. I'm hoping for a little imaginative synthesis tonight and could frankly do without the competition. Beat it!

Flashback fades into second flashback.

scene ten Flashback to 1966

Edina's childhood home. Very small kitchen table. Mother is serving Edina and Patsy some rather dull food.

Mother *(Singing along to the radio.)* La, la, la, la. *(To Patsy.)* Is your mother not feeding you, dear?

Edina Mum, you know what she's like.

Mother Can't have you turning into a great gangly wotsit. Skinny belinki long-legs, big banana feet. *(Hands her some nice pudding.)*

Patsy Thanks, Mrs M.

Flashback fades into next flashback.

scene eleven Flashback to 1977

Corner of an old people's home. Patsy's mother, very old, is sitting in chair with blanket over knees. Patsy is visiting.

Patsy's mother Look at you, all grief and resentful care. Here I am in this place of old age and pallid diseases with these so-called nurses, just gropers of old bones. You come here and hang breathless around me hoping I'm going to die. Denied even my intellectual liberty, allowed only two Barbara Cartland's a month. The tyranny of children.

Patsy Oh, for god's sake, just die.

scene twelve Saffron's Bedroom

Patsy is now sitting on bed next to Saffron.

Patsy She died soon after that. The last thing she said to me was 'Why? Why have we always been fighting? Why have our swords always been locked in battle?'

Saffron What did you say?

Patsy I said 'we've had locked shields not swords'.

Saffron That's very sad.

Patsy I know. *(Secretly triumphant.)*

Saffron Look . . .

Patsy *(Too quickly.)* Yes?

Saffron I . . .

Patsy Yes . . .

Saffron *(Stands up.)* I'll make a deal with you.

Patsy Okay.

Saffron I'll do your makeover thing on two conditions.

Patsy Name them.

Saffron You move out of this house into a hotel, and you allow Mum to have a boyfriend.

Patsy Done. *(Goes to exit.)* Ring your grandmother. We need an old woman as well.

scene thirteen Edina's Kitchen

It is six a.m. Patsy is slumped over the kitchen table. Edina comes down the stairs. Both look the worse for wear.

Edina Patsy, wake up. Patsy, wake up. *(Patsy lifts her head. Her face is red and her hair is flat where she has been lying.)*

Patsy What time is it?

Edina It's six o'clock in the morning. Don't even begin to even think about it.

Patsy sniffs smelling salts.

Edina Okay. So what time did you get to sleep?

Patsy Oh about three a.m.

Edina Yeah, I tried about midnight and then I took some pills about one.

Patsy It's so long since I remember going to sleep, instead of passing out. How do people do it?

Edina How did you get on with the makeover thing?

Patsy Well, your mother's fine. She'll wear what she's put in. But that bitch daughter of yours. I've tried everything. Won't wear one Galliano.

Edina Look, I know this is going to sound rather odd, but have you tried saying 'please'?

Patsy What?

Edina I don't know why, but it often works with Saffy. Give it a go, babe.

Patsy I can't.

Edina Just do it. It's over pretty quick.

Patsy No, I mean, I can't say it. Don't make me say it. It's difficult for me.

Edina Try. Just say 'Please, Saffy, wear the Galliano'. Then smile.

Patsy *(Tries, but gives up.)* I can't smile like that. If I smile I'm lost, I'm like a child. You do it.

Edina Is everything else organized?

Patsy Yes, yes, yes.

Edina You know what you're going to say?

Patsy Yes.

Edina Got a catchphrase?

Patsy A what?

Edina A little saying . . . something to sum up with.

Patsy Eddie, it's a cinch. I could do it in my sleep.

Mother and Saffron enter.

Mother Come on, come on. We're due in makeup at seven.

Saffron Are you coming, Mum? Aren't you with Jean-Pierre today?

Edina No, darling. They're shooting a video today.

Saffron Won't you need to be at the shop?

Edina I can be. I'm coming. Patsy has something to ask you, Saffy.

Edina looks at Patsy. Patsy shakes her head.

Edina Go on, Pats. I won't look.

Patsy takes Saffron aside.

Patsy Now, listen. I . . . *(She struggles to spit the word out.)* . . . Please wear the Galliano.

Saffron Okay. Come on. Let's get going.

Mother I wonder if Aunty Clare Rayner will be on, answering problems.

Patsy No, I'm on.

Mother She may be on, too. I do hope so. I'm always writing to Clare.

Edina What about? There's nothing wrong with you.

Mother I did once think I had that disease . . . You know the one that you get when you're old. What's it called? The one that makes you forget everything? What is it again?

Edina Alzheimers.

Mother Is it? I don't remember.

Saffron Come on. We're going to be late.

Mother *(Looking at Patsy.)* Strange that the makeover should be on us.

scene fourteen TV A.M. Studio
'After Nine' is happening with regular presenter, Kathy.

Kathy ... and coming up later on ... After ... er ... nine, our regular doctor, Shirley Jones, our 'Doc Spot', where our regular or actually not-so-regular, we've not seen him for ... oh, yes, we have ... He was here yesterday ... Our regular doctor will be answering some problems of his own, too. Look forward to that. And of course now ... this ... a ... letter. Yes, 'letter spot'. I've been sent a letter here from Mr Cowan and he says ... *(Cheerily.)* ... that he has just lost his dear lady wife. 'She was a lovely woman', he writes and 'when she died he felt a light had gone out'. Oh! *(She realizes it's a sad letter.)* Aaaaaah! He felt a light had gone out! *(Continues reading.)* She loved flowers. Aaaaah! But, on the bright side, I expect there were a lot of lovely floral tributes at the funeral.

scene fifteen Side of TV Studio
Edina and Patsy are huddled together. Patsy is waiting to go on.

Edina How are you feeling?

Patsy I'm not nervous.

scene sixteen Sofa Area in TV Studio
Kathy is now sitting on sofa.

Kathy Later, we'll be talking to the sports personality of the year.

Patsy A contradiction in terms.

Kathy And . . . now we come to the spot that is always one of my favourites. It is, of course, 'fashion spot'.

Patsy's hand comes in from the side and grabs Kathy's collar to check the label.

Kathy And let's welcome our guest fashion expert this week, from *Ella* magazine, Patsy Stone.

Patsy *(Very nervous.)* Hi. Yes. Cheers. Thanks a lot.

Kathy So. Now. You've done our fashion spot, makeover spot this week. How did you get on?

Patsy Ya. Yes, well. Really very well.

Kathy You took two ordinary members of the public and made their dreams come true?

Patsy That's right.

Studio assistant takes cigarette from her hand.

Kathy I think we've got a photo of our two 'makeover spotters' . . . Have we? Is there a . . . photo . . . ?

Photo comes up of baby with saucepan on its head.

Kathy No . . .

Picture flashes up of Mother and Saffron looking normal.

Kathy There we are! So, a bit of work to be done there.

Patsy *(Frozen with fear.)* Yes, cheers, thanks a lot.

Kathy Let's have a look at them now.

Saffron walks out and sits on the couch.

Kathy Look, a lovely young lady.

Mother walks out and models her clothes. Both look over-fashionable and ridiculous.

Kathy Oh, here's someone of more mature years, not afraid, obviously, to wear bright colours in the evening of her life. Take the weight off your feet, dearie.

Mother Is Clare here?

Kathy No. She went with the franchise.

scene seventeen Edina's Kitchen

Edina, Patsy, Mother and Saffron are watching a video of the programme.

Saffron Never have I been so embarrassed and that's saying something after living with my mother for eighteen years.

Kathy *(On Screen.)* Well, they're not exactly workaday outfits. I mean, you'd feel a bit of a fool wearing them in your local supermarket.

Patsy *(In Kitchen.)* That's not the point, you stupid bitch.

Patsy *(On Screen.)* Yes. Cheers. Thanks a lot.

Kathy *(On Screen.)* Let's ask our guinea pigs how they feel about the outfits.

Patsy *(In Kitchen.)* No, don't. Don't talk to them.

Mother *(In Kitchen.)* Too late now, dear.

Mother *(On Screen.)* Well, I'm an M & S fan myself.

Kathy *(On Screen.)* So am I. You know where you are with M & S. Well, thank you for coming along. Yes, really lovely, if a bit way out for me.

Patsy *(On Screen.)* Can I just say . . .

Patsy *(In Kitchen.)* This is a good bit. Listen. *(Turns up volume.)*

162
163

Patsy *(On Screen.)* You can never have enough … hats, gloves and shoes.

Kathy *(On Screen.)* Well, absolutely lovely. Another good tip from our fashion expert. Later on, from 9:00 till 9:03 we're having an in-depth look at acute schizophrenia. And, of course, after Lizzy, what else but Youthenasia. We will be talking to people who pulled the plug on their mothers. *(To Mother.)* So, watch out. And now over to Eureka for the weather. Eureka.

Patsy *(On Screen.)* Cheers. Thanks a lot.

The TV is switched off.

Mother I think it went very well, dear.

Patsy Do you? Yes? Eddy?

Edina You were great, sweetie.

Saffron Mum! Don't humour her. She stunk.

Patsy Listen you, they offered me a job before I left.

Saffron It was only doing the weather, Patsy. Mum, have you spoken to Jean-Pierre? There was a message on the machine from him.

Edina I'm not going to see him any more, darling. Pats and I talked it through last night. What with the shop and his job, it's not really practical.

Saffron glares at Patsy.

Saffron Get out! You can at least keep one half of the deal.

Patsy Look, you did the telly, I'm not moving out.

Saffron Have you no honour?

Mother Lost that at fourteen from what I heard. I knew the boy.

Saffron storms out.

ABSOLUTELY fab

Edina *(To Patsy.)* How did you persuade Saffy to do it, Pats?

Patsy Oh, you know. Gave her the old story about my mother being a tyrant, not being loved and nursing her through her old age. Bla, bla, bla.

Edina But that's true.

Patsy *(Pauses.)* Damn!

scene eighteen Edina's Kitchen

Edina What are you up to tonight, Pats?

Patsy I'm seeing the publisher again, darling, just to be safe.

Edina Good idea, sweetie. I mean, even Amanda de Cadenet would remember the word 'accessories'.

164
165